VAN ISHED LIVES

VANISHED LIVES

A TRUE TALE
OF
OLD MANCHESTER

Alan Richardson

HEB ☼ HUMANITIES-EBOOKS

First published by Humanities-Ebooks
Tirril Hall, Penrith, Cumbria, CA10 2JE in January 2015

This paperback is available from Lulu.com

ISBN 978-1-84760-352-4 Paperback
ISBN 978-1-84760-353-1 Kindle

To the memory of

Ellen, Alice, John and Richard Richardson

Acknowledgements

The author wishes to thank Mr Stephen Kent for permission to publish the photographs of John Hall and his wife (page 84) and the Francis Frith Collection for the photograph of Piccadilly, Manchester (page 75). Miss T. Szczepanik kindly helped with finding certain information on John Richardson (1798–1869) He is also indebted to Dr Richard Gravil for invaluable aid with the preparation of the manuscript for publication.

Contents

FAMILY MYTHS

Why research a family's history? Why bother reading someone else's family history? There is only one answer – for pleasure. I have enjoyed researching the lives of my ancestors and perhaps you will enjoy reading the results.

I was born on May 31st 1940 at the Salvation Army's Crossley Hospital, Pollard Street, Ancoats, Manchester, into a working class family. On that day, 69,000 British and French soldiers were lifted from the beaches at Dunkirk by the Royal Navy; it was our nation's darkest hour and my 21 year-old mother, fearing that German paratroopers might interrupt her delivery, berated my father for having placed her in such a predicament. Thus, I first breathed air in a country facing defeat and humiliation. But my folks, Mancunians bred and born, were proud of their country and their city and, like millions of others, were grimly prepared to fight it out.

In my early years I learned of their immediate ancestors whose lives had been inextricably bound up with Manchester's fortunes. My father, Richard, was born in Kinlock Street, Bradford, in August 1912; and my mother, Alma (née) Keeling, was born at 27, Haddon Street, Beswick, in September 1918. Their forebears were factory workers who avoided poverty and early death only by luck and unremitting toil. Sickness and unemployment were their ever present terrors. My mother's father, Frederick Keeling, was a foundry worker who had died in his fifties in 1934 after years of unemployment and poverty - not the statistical poverty of the 21st century, but the absolute poverty defined by not having enough food, shoes or clothes, and living in a ramshackle insanitary dwelling where children died of cold and disease. Lizzie, his wife, worked in the mill whenever she could and, unsurprisingly, her life's experiences made her the gloomy old woman I remember.

My father's family were more fortunate by dint of his father, John Richardson, having a modestly well-paid job with Messrs Smith and Forrest, tar distillers, at Holt Town, Ancoats. His mother's people (Haworths and Reids) had lived in Ancoats since the 1830s when the Reids had arrived from Ireland. Both my parents' families had their myths; the Keelings a saga of bad luck, with the bread-winners in two generations dying young. By contrast, the Richardsons had been a well-to-do family that had owned the Mosley Hotel on Piccadilly. Their myths were of legal skulduggery and feckless "black sheep." My great-grandfather was named Robert Bradbury Richardson and his sister, Polly, clung to her shrunken gentility in retirement at Victoria Park, bitterly claiming that she and her brother had been swindled out of a fortune. This myth, garbled with re-telling, was enlivened in the 1930s, when the Manchester Corporation sought my grandfather's permission to remove certain pictures from the city art gallery. My Uncle John presumed they had belonged to the family and suspected the family fortune was hidden in a bank vault, waiting to be prised from some rascally lawyer's grasp. He and his sisters remembered the plentiful whiskers of the wealthy patriarchs depicted in two gilt-framed oil portraits that had clung to the wall of their grandfather's tiny living room in Beswick. And there was a large family Bible with faded calf-skin covers whose pages recorded some births, deaths and marriages back to the late 1700s. Another enigmatic heir-loom was a stout, leather-bound volume printed at Blackburn in 1799; *Hurd's Religions of the World*. It bore a signature on the fly-leaf, "J Richardson's book 1800."

These Richardson myths intrigued me and when I was about sixteen (1956) I began to collect such information as I could. It was slow work until the age of the internet; but eventually I could explain them. The emerging saga with its sub-plots were worthy of a 19th century novel. It involved feuds, love affairs, celebrities and great melodramas. The background was the harsh reality of 19th century Manchester life with its perennial promise of wealth and equally perennial threats of sickness, destitution and untimely death.

POOR BETTY

Cumberland Richardsons – Betty – Wigton paupers in the 1700s - John Richardson's birth and childhood.

Sometime about the year 1780, a young boy left his home in the small market town of Wigton about 12 miles south-west of Carlisle in Cumberland. He was fatherless and penniless, and but for the charity of the parish, he would have been bootless and coatless too. He was John Richardson, a name so common in the north of England that that it might be found in every parish from the Cheviots to the Mersey. It proclaimed a northern heritage and made a shadowy allusion to a remote and noble ancestry, though I doubt John knew much about it.

Richardson means *son of Richard*, and originated in Europe's remote ages. The element *ric* occurs in several ancient languages and meant a "powerful chief"; one "rich" in talents as much as in wealth. It was popular with the Normans, those Vikings who settled in northern France before conquering England in 1066. In the late 1120s, the Norman king, Henry I, ejected the Scots from Cumberland and built a new castle in the ruined Roman city of Carlisle. Among the Normans who garrisoned the district was a Richard *le Ridere,* (rider or knight) of the de Tilliol family.[1] In 1130, he held two nearby manors which his descendants kept until 1435 when his male line died out. To one manor he gave his name, *Rickerby,* a local Norse rendering of Richard's village. The de Tilliols acquired land west of Carlisle and the outlines of one of their fortified towers, or *mottes,* can be seen beside the Carlisle – Cockermouth road at Mealsgate near Wigton. Richard remained a popular name with them, Richard son of Richard occurring in their records. However, by the time surnames were coming into use, the prestige of Richard le Ridere was forgotten, and by the time documents became common, the Richardsons were mainly yeomen and tenant farmers scattered about the county. In the 1750s, there were seven Richardson families in Wigton and Caldbeck, some yeomen, some more humble.[2] It is from a native of Wigton, a certain William Richardson, born in the early 1700s, that John took his surname.[3] But he was not of William's blood.

In April 1743, William Richardson married the 19 year old Elizabeth Holmes. She was popularly called Betty and episodes of her sad life can be glimpsed from snippets in our family Bible and the Wigton parish records. The crucial link occurred on April 19th 1769, when Betty's infant son was christened at the Wigton church. He was two and half years old.[4] The register notes, "John, son of Elizabeth Richardson, spur." i.e., illegitimate.

Betty was forty two, a widow and a pauper who had depended on the parish for some years. In 1763, she had 2/6 for a petticoat and clogs for her daughter and in 1764 four shillings a week for herself and four children. William may have died or simply disappeared, perhaps pressed into the army or navy, but he must have been a Wigton native because parishes supported only their own poor. Indeed, poor outsiders could be whipped and sent on their way. The Wigton parish register does not record any further christenings of their children, so they may have moved away, with Betty and the children returning after William's demise.

Poor Betty struggled on handouts until her death 20 years later. Several of the poor records mention her house-rent paid to Jonathon Grainger and a shop-keeper named Jonathon Kay. A poorhouse was built in Wigton in the 1760s,[5] but throughout 1766 Betty received 9d a week for rent. This outdoor relief was based on the poor law of Elizabeth I and was quite humane by the standards of the time. Indeed, the rate-payers who financed it came to regard it as too humane. On the other hand, they knew the paupers personally and divided them into the "deserving" and the "undeserving." Betty seems to have been regarded as a genuine case. The reformed Parliament of 1832, reflecting the attitudes of the newly enfranchised middle class, replaced this humane system with the infamous workhouses that punished the poor for their poverty.

Many of Wigton's paupers were sick and Betty earned small fees from nursing them. The records mention these services; for example, in August 1764 she had a shilling for "waiting of Gordon's wife." In December, "Nurse Richardson's daughter" received nine pence, and then ten shillings "for stays, gown and linning (i.e. linen) and a shift." She is variously called Betty, Elizabeth, Eliza and "Nurse." But nursing was not then a respected profession, but degrading work chiefly done by poor women. Some had babies so they could suckle the children of richer women. The literature of the day often depicts them as ignorant, loose-living tipplers and Charles Dickens's Mrs Gamp is a good example. This view did not change for another hundred years.

Was Betty such a person? It is impossible to say, but at Christmas 1765 she conceived our John. Whether this was due to a love affair or a desperate measure to produce a saleable baby-milk supply, it is likely to have followed a Cumbrian "merry neet" when dancing to the drum, fiddle and flute usually lead to amours. There are no clues as to the child's father though, intriguingly, the overseer of the parish poor was a certain John Richardson. Throughout her pregnancy Betty received money and when confined in September 1766, the parish paid, "Elizabeth Trickle for delivering nurse, 3/-" and gave her £1 "for lying in one month." In January 1767, she had cash to clothe her child and four shillings worth of cloth, and was then sick for most of the year. In 1768, she had money for her "childor" (dialect form of children) and 3/6 for stockings. Her life was undoubtedly very hard and may explain why young John was not christened until he was two and a half.

So here we have our little boy, a Richardson by reason of his mother having married William, but sprung from the Holmes line by a father unknown. The Holmes name derives from the Wigton area; the *holmes* being the higher grounds in the former marshland behind the Solway shore. The Solway plainsmen were a variant on the robber clans that ruled the border lands; herdsmen and shepherds who dwelled in hovels of earth and furze, known as "clay dabbins." They were an ancient race who told the tales and sang the ballads of bygone days beside their winter hearths; of raids and trysts, of treachery and of valour.

It seems that despite John's birth Betty was regarded as a deserving case, for at "a publick meeting" on July 4th 1774 she was advanced 9/- for her half-year's rent. And somehow young John obtained a basic education; possibly at the charity school held on weekdays in the Wigton church.[6] He certainly became a literate, hard-working and presentable lad.

The fate of Betty's other children is not known. She had a daughter Susannah, known as "Zana", who, with her brother, received clothes from the parish. In September 1777, Wilfrid Lawson was paid "for making Bette Richardson son a coate." According to a law of 1690, this would have carried a patch on the left shoulder bearing the letters "PW"; the "P" standing for "pauper" and the "W" for "Wigton." Its purpose was to grant the pauper permission to beg and remind him of his status. In March 1777, the overseers arranged for a poor thirteen year-old boy, Ephraim Richardson, to be bound as an apprentice husbandman to a Mr Frith of Sebergham, a hamlet about eight miles away.[7] This lad may have been our John's half-brother. His biblical name chimes with that of Betty's daughter, Susannah.

By 1778, Betty was lame, but the parish records after 1779 are lost and her next mention is of her burial from the poorhouse in June 1787, at the age of 63. By then, John was 21 and had almost certainly left Wigton. Was Betty an incompetent, loose woman or a desperately unlucky victim of widowhood, deceit and sickness? I prefer to conclude from the resolution of the "publick meeting" of July 1774, that she was regarded as "the deserving poor." Moreover, John named his first born daughter, Betsey, after her, just as his first son was named Richard, after his father-in-law. When Betsey died in infancy, the next daughter was also named Betsy. Here is a clue that John loved his mother.

It is certain that as soon as John could earn his living, probably at the age of 13, like young Ephraim, the parish overseers would have found him a job. I suspect he went as a servant to an inn-keeper at Carlisle where he would have begun to learn the menial crafts of cleaning boots and emptying chamber pots. He could not have been a strapping lad, having been reared on gruel and oatcakes baked on a slate on an open fire. We can imagine him embracing his mother before setting out upon the high road. Neither could have dreamt that his daughters and grand-daughters would marry into the families of rich India merchants, London publishers, Manchester industrialists and the Belgian gentry.

THE INNKEEPER

Stage coaches and post boys – Chorley - The Geneva Bible - Richard and Alice Hough – John's marriage and family – The Royal Oak– Hurd's "Religions of the World" – Manchester.

We can imagine John tramping along the old Roman road from Wigton to Carlisle with a sack over his head to keep off the rain, his boots in tatters and his ragged coat with the hated "PW" patch torn from it. If he went as a servant to a Carlisle inn, he would have come into contact with the stage-coach business, then expanding rapidly thanks to the new turnpike roads and improved coaches. At that time, long distance coach travel depended on the "posting" system by which private coaches were kept moving despite their horses becoming tired. They travelled in stages, with the coach owners hiring horses from inn-keepers along their way. At the end of each run, tired horses were replaced by a fresh team and the coach continued on its way. The teams were handled by "post-boys" who rode pillion and returned with the horses to their home inn after they had been fed and rested. The Manchester historian, J.T. Slugg, recalled seeing gangs of post boys at Garstang in the summer, when large numbers of coaches passed through to the Lakes and Scotland. The boys wore short red, or blue, jackets with brass buttons, buckskin breeches and top-boots.[8] Commercial coach operators adapted the system to maintain regular services.

John may have become a post-boy and so moved to Lancashire, because in the early 1790s, he was living at Chorley, a large village between Bolton and Preston. It had one main street with the parish church of St Lawrence at its northern end and its largest inn, the Royal Oak, a few hundred yards to the south. Since John became its landlord in 1800, it is highly likely that he was employed there in the 1790s.

On June 11th 1793, John married Margaret Hough, the 22 year-old daughter of a weaver, Richard Hough, and his wife, Alice, at Chorley church.[9] The Houghs were local people and Richard was the devout owner of a large Geneva Bible published in Edinburgh in 1777 by the Society for the Propagation of Christian Knowledge (SPCK) and it became our family Bible. The Geneva Bible was translated from the Greek by John Frederick Ostervald (b.1663) of Neufchatel, Switzerland, and then put into English. The SPCK's activities provoked one of William Cobbett's outbursts against the Church of England of his day. On learning that the king had instructed the clergy to beg their congregations to send donations to the SPCK, via a certain London merchant, he wrote:

> *What! The church and all its clergy put in motion to get money from the people to send to one Joshua Watson, a wine merchant, or, late a wine merchant, in Mincing Lane, Fenchurch Street, London, in order that the said wine merchant may apply the money to the "promoting of Christian Knowledge!" What! All the deacons, priests, curates perpetual, vicars, rectors, prebends, doctors, deans, archdeacons and fathers in God, right reverend and most reverend; all! Yea all, engaged in getting money together to send to a wine merchant that he may lay it out in the promoting of Christian knowledge <u>in their own flocks</u>.*[10]

John and Margaret's first child, Betsey, was born in 1794, but died the next year.[11] Their first son, Richard, arrived in November 1795 and young John followed in January 1798. Another daughter, Alice, named after Margaret's mother, was born in March 1800. In that year, when John was 34, the tenancy of the Royal Oak became vacant when John Crowe, passed it to H. Darby, who quitted almost at once.[12] Darby's departure in May allowed John to step in. The fact that he could raise the necessary capital and credit suggests he had learned his trade well and impressed potential backers.

The inn was a plain brick building with a thatched roof, sash windows and four tall chimneys, the venue for vestry meetings and other social functions. Its owners, the Leigh brothers, cotton spinners, had

The Royal Oak at Chorley drawn from a photo of 1937

recently bought it from the Stoneyhurst estate.[13] Outside the front door stood a large oak tree, probably planted in 1660 to celebrate the Restoration of the monarchy that the inn's name commemorated.[14] Inside was an old oak chest dating from 1704. It was the posting house for the mail coaches and in view of the inn's growing importance, the Leighs promised to make improvements. There was stabling for 44 horses, at least ten posting teams, housing for four coaches and a 28-acre farm to provide hay, oats and dairy produce.[15] The coaches drew off the main street through an archway into the yard where the horses were changed whilst the passengers were refreshed. A photograph of 1887 suggests the inn changed little over the years, other than having slates replace the thatch. It was demolished in 1937 to make way for an ugly red-brick inn and a row of shops.

John and Margaret began with their own improvements, adding a coffee shop and a reading room.[16] The Chorley tontine was declared there in August 1800 and on September 20th there was an auction sale."[17] Many others followed.[18]

Richard Hough died in January 1806 and was buried in Chorley churchyard. His tombstone lies near that of John's family; both now flagstones outside the church's eastern end. He left his Bible to Margaret and on the 22nd, she recorded the fact on the inside cover. John also signed his name in a bold script with flourishing capitals that hint at a confident man. He seems to have shared Hough's piety, since in 1800 he had acquired a volume of Dr Richard Hurd's *Religions of the World*, printed at Blackburn in 1799. It is a scholarly tome written in quaint and ponderous prose, but I suspect John had little time for reading. In these busy years, John and Margaret had more children, though James, born in 1802, died twelve months later. The next five lived to maturity: Betsey (b. 1803): James (b. 1805): Margaret (b. 1808): Mary (b. 1810): Ann (b. 1813).

These were the years of the Napoleonic War when trade was badly affected by the closure of continental ports to British goods. There was much unemployment and poverty in the industrial towns and by 1811 these woes forced John to slash his posting fees. He announced it in *The Manchester Courier and Lancashire General Advertiser* of June 26th 1811.

> ROYAL OAK INN, CHORLEY: *John Richardson begs to return his most sincere thanks to the Nobility, Gentry and Public in general, for the liberal support he has experienced since his commencement in business, and respectfully informs them that he has reduced the price of posting from 1s 6d to 8d per mile. He assures the public it shall be his particular study in every department of his concerns as Inn-keeper, to merit a continuation of their favours.* [19]

In 1811, young Richard and John were 16 and 13 respectively and almost certainly helped with the posting. Perhaps Slugg saw them in their brass-buttoned splendour at Garstang. But John wished them to be educated and they may have attended Chorley Grammar School, a mean 27 x 18 feet building behind the Royal Oak, or may have crammed their lessons at one of Chorley's private "academies." [20] All the children must have watched, perhaps with some envy, the local worthies in their finery trouping into the Royal Oak for the functions that marked Chorley's social year.

John and Margaret ran the Royal Oak for 13 years, during which successive mediocre British governments grappled with the Napoleonic menace. In response to the French emperor's trade embargo, Britain enforced a vigorous naval blockade of European ports, but otherwise stumbled from one fiasco to another. But in 1813, after Napoleon's disaster in Russia and Wellington's victories in Spain, the Europeans threw off French domination and opened their ports to British goods. The long silent Lancashire mills were suddenly busy. By this time John had probably brought the Royal Oak to its maximum return and paid off his initial capital investment. To meet his future hopes for his children he needed a bigger business, which meant moving to a bigger town. In February 1813, their last child, Ann, was born and in June they moved to Manchester.[21]

MANCHESTER

Manchester in 1813 – Robert Southey and child labour – The Moseley Arms Inn – Market Street - A family death – The Peterloo Massacre – Gentleman John – Robert Bradbury – John's prosperity – Manchester stage-coaches – Moseley Arms guests – Anne Lister of Shibden – Marriages – Robert Bent and William Barnfield – Margaret's death – Young John.

In 1813 Manchester was a new phenomenon; the world's first industrial city and the wonder of the age. It had grown steadily for more than a century but within John's lifetime the mechanisation of the textile industry had turned it from a sleepy market town into a thriving metropolis. Cotton, imported through Liverpool, was shipped to Manchester and its satellite towns by river and canal and there turned into cloth. The first mills had been small, water-powered factories beside the Pennine streams but they were now being replaced by factories of six or more floors, crammed with steam-powered machines over which men, women and children toiled in stifling heat. When John was a child, Manchester's population was 40,000. It had risen to 95,000 by 1800 and in 1813 there were 64,000 textile workers alone.[22] From the heights above the Irwell from where the family probably first glimpsed their new home, there was a pleasing prospect of green fields, orchards and woodlands that was seared by a rash of new brick buildings and a forest of tall chimneys pouring out a filthy haze.

Manchester had first grown up around a prehistoric site near a Roman fort at the confluence of the rivers Medlock and Irwell. The road going north-east from the fort (the fore-runner of Deansgate) was met, at a 'T' junction, by Market Street which connected to the London Road at Ardwick. The town grew by ribbon develop-

The Top of Market Street in the 1820s.

The Moseley Arms Inn is probably the building with the royal coat of arms over
the door dating from its time as the Royal Oak. If not, it was the next further away.
From John Ralston's *Views of the Ancient Buildings in Manchester* (1823–25).

ment along these roads and in 1813 many old half-timbered buildings remained jumbled together along narrow winding side lanes,
with passages and courts running in all directions. The mediaeval
Collegiate church was the hub of a conservative community that had
sympathised with the Jacobite cause, and when John's mother was a
young woman in Cumberland. Bonnie Prince Charlie had recruited
200 Manchester men for his rebellion. Sixty years later, factories,
warehouses and fine villas were encroaching into the greenery of
Chorlton-on-Medlock, Ardwick and Ancoats. Didsbury, Withington,
Clayton and Droylsden were still out in the country, but the black tide
had begun its outward spread. Sir Arthur Bryant has described the
impact of the new industry on the landscape.[23]

> *The trout streams were being poisoned by dye vats and the
> valleys studded with smoke stacks; the willows and hazels of
> the Irk blackened and laid waste, the groves of birch, wild rose
> and rowan and green hills with classical names and haunting
> rustic deities - Babylon Brow and Stony Knows - desecrated
> by money grinders.*

In 1808, Robert Southey visited a Manchester mill with one of
those money grinders.[24]

> *He took us to one of the great cotton manufactories, showed
> us the number of children who were at work there, and dwelt
> in great delight on the infinite good which resulted from
> employing them at so early an age. I listened without contra-
> dicting him, for who would lift up his voice against Diana in
> Ephesus? 'You see these children, sir' said he, 'they get their
> bread almost as soon as they can walk about, and by the time
> they are about seven or eight years old bring in money. There
> is no idleness amongst us; - they come at five in the morning;
> we allow them half an hour for breakfast, and an hour for
> dinner; they leave work at six and another set relieves them
> for the night; the wheels never stand still.' It would have been
> in vain to argue had I been disposed to it. I thought of cities in
> Arabian romance, where all the inhabitants were enchanted:*

here Commerce is the queen witch, and I had no talisman strong enough to disenchant those who were daily drinking of the golden cup of her charms.

After two centuries, the Industrial Revolution is seen as a *good thing*, as it was at the time by those who gained from it. In the 1830s, Macaulay, a liberal and humane man, argued with lofty confidence that the factory system had greatly improved material condition of the working class, and would continue to do so. He cited the statistics to prove it. [25] But he overlooked a simple truth; the improvements detectable over decades were accompanied by episodes of poverty that destroyed millions. Who would willingly suffer privation in his day so that his great grand-children *might* prosper in theirs?

Whilst in Manchester, Southey stayed at the Bridgewater Arms and his comments on the service he received give a clue as to why John thought he could succeed in the town.

In these large manufacturing towns inns have neither the cleanliness nor the comfort we find in smaller places. In the country there is a civility about the people of the house, which, though you know hospitality is their trade, seem to show something of the virtue. Here all is hurry and bustle; customers must come in the way of trade, and they care not whether you are pleased or not.[26]

The family's new home was the Moseley Arms Inn at 63, Market Street.* It was at the hub of the town's stagecoach business and having secured the lease, John was established by June 1813.[27] The inn was a four storey building facing onto the pavement on the south side at the upper end, below the Bridgewater Arms and extending into Fountain Street. Five years earlier it had been the Royal Oak with "coach houses, extensive stabling, yard, coach offices, buildings, etc." but was renamed in 1809.[28] It was probably the former home of David Holt, a Quaker cotton-spinner and philanthropist whose factories in Ancoats gave that locality the name of Holt Town.[29] According to

---

* There was no consistency in the spelling of *Moseley*, or *Mosley*, in the 19th century. I have adhered to *Moseley* except with quotations.

Swindells, "…the Mosley was an important coaching house, Charles Scudamore running coaches to London daily. His announcement declared that the coaches performed the journey in 29 hours, carried four inside and were well-lighted and guarded all the way." [30]

The street outside was described by Mrs Banks in *The Manchester Man*.[31]

> *Market Street … was then Market Street Lane, a confused medley of shops and private houses, varying from the low and rickety black and white tenement of no pretensions, to the fine mansion with an imposing frontage, and ample space before. But the thoroughfare was in places so very narrow that two vehicles could not pass, and pedestrians on the footpath were compelled to take refuge in doorways from the muddy wheels which threatened damage to dainty garments; and the whole was ill-paved and worse lighted.*

Though the move was financially wise, there was an awful price to pay. In those days, people moving to the town from the country, especially the young, were exposed to diseases against which they had no immunity. This was particularly true of tuberculosis. On January 7th 1816, Richard died at the age of twenty-two.[32] This must have been a calamity. We know nothing of the young man, save that he was named after his grandfather Hough and probably held that place in parental affection that younger siblings often resent. He was buried at Chorley.[33]

Nor was Manchester a happy place. Despite the end of the war the town was much agitated by starving workers who rioted and broke into shops for food. Among their leaders were those who argued there could be no real improvement in their conditions until Parliament were reformed. The government was in the hands of landed men who, at best, might be kind to their village poor and humane enough to abolish the slave-trade in 1807, but blind to the problems of free working-men coping with slumps and greedy masters – and after the horrors of the French Revolution, they would not yield power. A snobbish young Yorkshire woman staying at the Moseley Arms in September 1818 noted the town was full of soldiers who had been brought in to intimidate workers whom she thought well paid and without any reason to complain.[34] In that year a mass march on London by workers known as the "blanketeers" was forcibly broken up, so their leaders planned a large protest meeting to be held at Manchester in August 1819. To ensure good order and avoid the slur of being called a rabble, they drilled in companies like soldiers; whereupon the authorities took fright.

The result was the Peterloo Massacre when cavalry, under orders from the jittery magistrates, charged a peaceful crowd of 65,000 on St Peter's fields, about half a mile from the Moseley Arms. There were a great many casualties, including women and children, but the shamefaced Manchester authorities brazenly faced down censure. First, they met at the police station and then, to cloak their credentials and pretend they represented moderate public opinion, they withdrew to the Star Inn, Deansgate, and passed a resolution thanking the government for the soldiers' services. There was an immediate outcry and a petition deploring the Star Inn resolution was soon signed by almost 5,000 people.[35] A John Richardson was listed among them.[36]

Richard's death meant that 18-year old John was now the eldest son and thus, according to custom, destined to take over the Moseley Arms one day. But John was a troublesome fellow and his succession was not a happy prospect. He was training to be a lawyer and in February 1818, just past his 20th birthday, he married Elizabeth, the 18 year-old daughter of a widow, Grace Hardcastle, at the Collegiate Church. Elizabeth's father, John, had been a cloth-dresser who died of "decay" in 1804.[37] John's youth hints at a hurried arrangement, and now the inn-keeper's son and probable former post-boy, described himself as a "gentleman" in the church register; and thus he posed for the rest of his life. Old John never suffered this conceit but, perhaps because of his own wretched childhood, he allowed his lad to indulge it. He gave the young man £1,300, about £100,000 at 2010 values, for a legal training, or a business, or to pay off debts, or perhaps for all three.[38] In 1821, a certain John Richardson of Manchester, a dealer in cotton, went bankrupt.[39] Gambling in cotton was a common way for rich young men to ruin themselves and our lad was to gain a reputation for financial incompetence. Whether or not he went bankrupt, young John acquired some legal training and in 1824 was appointed a commissioner of oaths for the northern counties. [40] He kept the royal warrant safe because it opened with the king addressing him as "gentleman" in words that have the timbre of bygone days.

> GEORGE the Fourth by the GRACE of GOD of the United Kingdom of GREAT BRTAIN & IRELAND King, DEFENDER of the FAITH, To our well-beloved John Richardson of Manchester in the County of Lancaster, Gentleman ….

It was signed by Sir Robert Dallas, Knight, on the 17th of June, "in the fourth year of our reign." [41] A note scribbled on the back states, "Mr Richardson – paid." For some years John practised the sober profession of a solicitor, but it was not to his taste. He was a dandy in the heyday of dandies, fast-living, hard-drinking and often vicious young men who dressed flashily and lounged about taverns and theatres like fighting cocks. Manchester's finest of this species was a celebrity named Robert Bradbury. Our John almost certainly knew him. Bradbury's *forte* was the pantomime; a genre newly introduced from Italy and appreciated by the whole public. Charles Dickens was a great admirer of the art.

Because of Gentleman John's later history, and particularly his naming a son after him, it is worth digressing into Bradbury's life. He was born in 1771 and brought up in Manchester where, as a boy, he practiced acrobatics on a piece of carpet laid on a tombstone in the churchyard next to his home.[42] He made his debut as a clown in Liverpool in the late 1700s,[43] and first appeared on the Manchester stage in 1802.[44] He was a gifted acrobat, stunt man and animal trainer. "He possessed prodigious strength and … his feats were … calculated to terrify than to amuse his auditors." [45] His most famous stunt was to lie down with a blacksmith's anvil on his chest, upon which three burly men banged with sledge hammers.[46] He was "a great favourite with the public … passionately fond of dress and jewellery." [47] In 1803, he temporally ousted the great Grimaldi from Saddlers Wells with an act involving a pig and he later kept a pet bear.[48] He could balance on 10 foot crutches atop a ladder and took great risks to shock his audiences.[49] Extrovert, cheeky and flamboyant, and known as the "Brummel of clowns," he sported "dandy fashions," and was "ambitious of the society of gentleman", tried to talk posh and kept a two-horse carriage.[50] "Mr Francis Astley of Dukinfield, Cheshire, paid him much attention … and made him a present of a gold snuff box, value forty pounds." [51] "But beneath the veneer," wrote McConnell Stott, "lay a reputation for brawling and bullying" – and he could be very vulgar – upsetting audiences for whose feelings he did not care. His first employer, Ryley, described him as "… athletic, active and possessed … of considerable pugilistic skill" and recounted his entering a Glasgow inn where his magnificent presence induced the guests to presume he was the Duke of Buccleugh.[52]

> *…a tall athletic person entered the room, and commanded the attention of all present. His hair was somewhat sandy, and rather thin on the forepart of his head; to provide for this deficiency, a sprinkling of powder was applied; the lower part of his face seemed buried in immense whiskers, the dog ears, as they are sometimes called, a stiff neck collar, reaching nearly to the cheek bones around which a handsome silk handkerchief, a la Belcher,[53] terminated in the best exquisite Bond-street knot. Beneath a light drab coat, made in the first hunting frock fashion, appeared a pink and white striped waistcoat, with a sham or two of blue and red satin, peeping from under the breast, doe skin small clothes, white top boots, gilt spurs and an immense cluster of gold seals attached to an elegant gold chain, drawn through the waistcoat button-hole. Thus equipped, he stood before us, rubbing his chain with the silver handle of a neat horse whip. All was silence…*

In 1805, Bradbury began the *Chatham Street Circus* in Manchester.[54] Then in 1809, he re-opened the theatre in Fountain Street, re-named it the *Amphitheatre,* and put on variety shows with singing, dancing, acrobatic performances and displays of horsemanship. But the venture failed so he changed the format.[55] Then his career met a set-back.

While at Portsmouth in 1809, he was involved in an incident which reveals either a great benevolence of character, or base cunning. Whilst in the company of an aristocratic army officer about to sail for India, he was robbed of a gold snuff box, possibly Francis Astley's gift. The Bow Street runners were called and the box was found in the officer's possession. To spare the noble family's disgrace, and at their request, Bradbury agreed to ignore the theft and claim that he had fabricated the accusation in a fit of madness. The police would not connive at this, but Bradbury's play-acting convinced them to drop the case. The noble family was most grateful and, Bradbury claimed later, paid him well for the imposture. Nevertheless, the officer cut his throat out of shame. Bradbury then entered an asylum, treating the whole business as a lucrative stunt. On his release, he appeared at Grimaldi's benefit show but was so vulgar that the audience hissed him off the stage. He then took up itinerant preaching until the hecklers drove him back to clowning. [56] He appeared at Bow Street in 1811 to refute a charge of theft of £45 from a Mr Croston, pleading that he had refused to pay an exorbitant fare for being conveyed from Portsmouth during his "illness." [57]

In January 1813, Bradbury opened in *Mother Goose* at Fountain Street, Manchester, where our young John probably first saw him. "After a mysterious interval of three years' duration, caused by serious illness and misfortune in the neighbourhood of Portsmouth.... the lovers of mirth in its most eccentric exuberance found a rich treat in his performances." [58] He starred in *Mother Goose* for several years in Manchester and at Drury Lane, London, and he claimed to have been the first to have put on this show at Manchester. [59]

Bradbury died penniless in his lodgings at Royal Row, Westminster, on July 21st 1831, aged 54. *The Gentleman's Magazine* described him as the eccentric "Bob Bradbury, the well-known clown" who once made £600 with one show at Dublin. [60] He was famous to his generation and his feats were recorded in several memoirs. Robert Southey, compared the essayist Hazlitt to him; – an acrobat on a high ladder, a "tumbling clown rather than a humorous one." He reminds us of Bradbury, "dancing upon stilts." [61] That young John admired this man enough to name a son after him fits with the other evidence that our lad was also a flashy spendthrift. Ryley's comment on Bradbury seems apt. "…his dashing appearance brought him on terms of intimacy with all the juvenile part of his visitors, many of whom were the younger sons of respectable families." [62]

In the 1820s, as the Moseley Arms Inn prospered, Cumberland John acquired friends among the Manchester worthies, including John Stuart, a surgeon of Oldham Street and Richard Smith, a paper maker, who had a mansion at Rusholme.[63] The Manchester hoteliers must have raised their standards since Southey's visit. William Cobbett, writing at Warminster in September 1826, noted, "This appears to be a sort of little Manchester. A very small Manchester, indeed; for it does not contain above ten or twelve thousand people, but it has all the flash of a Manchester, and the innkeepers and their people look and behave like Manchester fellows." He did not mean this as a complement, adding, "I was, I must confess, glad to find proofs of the irretrievable decay of the place…" and he went on to curse those responsible for the Peterloo massacre.[64]

In October 1821, Manchester's Court Leet appointed a certain John Richardson to be one of its officers. The court was the ancient government of the manor. The appointee may have been one of our Johns, though there were others in Manchester. With three or four others, this official was responsible for enforcing the local laws against "ingrossing, re-grating and forestalling." *Ingrossing* was making a monopoly. *Re-grating* was buying and selling in the same market, or as we would say, *playing* the market. *Forestalling* was cornering the market. All these activities, which are now regarded as more-or-less legitimate, were then regarded as against the public interest.

Cumberland John became a patron of the arts in 1824. The Manchester worthies knew that the Londoners, jealous of the northern upstarts' wealth, scorned them for lacking "culture." They responded by founding a society for the promotion of the fine arts in the town. Patrons were sought and for a donation of £42 (about £1,600 in modern money) John became a hereditary governor of the

Royal Manchester Institution which then built the city Art Gallery on Mosley Street.[65] At the age of 58, he was clearly active and about this time he had his portrait painted in oils. Cobbett reckoned innkeepers were much painted because poor artists often paid their bills in kind. This portrait survived, along with one of young John, until their destruction by the latter's grand-daughter in 1925.

The 1820s were the golden years of the stagecoach and the whole day at the Moseley Arms was taken up with arrivals and departures, as the 1815 Trades Directory shows.

Carlisle Coach	Carlisle	Daily at 6 am.
Royal Mail	Commercial Inn, Sheffield.	Daily at 7 am.
Express	Hen & Chickens, Birmingham	Daily at 8 am.
Defiance	Golden Lion, Leeds.	Mon-Sat at 12.30
Commercial	Angel Inn, Liverpool.	Daily at 10 am.
Telegraph	Liverpool	Daily at 2.30 pm.
Telegraph	White Horse, Fetter Lane, London	Daily at 4 pm.
Shuttle	Castle Inn, Preston	Daily at 4.30 pm.

As the volume of trade increased, John combined his coach ticket office with that of the Star Inn. In December and March 1828, *The Manchester Courier* carried notices for coaches running from the joint booking office, thus:

New Times	Carlisle	4.45 am
Regulator	Liverpool, Saracen's Head	5.15 am
Victory	Chester	5.45 am
Eclipse	Birmingham, Hen & Chickens	5.45 am
Champion	Nottingham	6.30 am
Butterfly	Preston, Red Lion & Black Bull	6.30 am
North Star	Kings Arms, Kendal	8.45 am
Wellington	Sheffield, Tontine & King's Hd.	9.30 am
Umpire	Leeds, White Horse	9.30 am
Defiance	Leeds, Golden Lion	11.45 am
Union	Wakefield, Stretford Arms	12.30 pm
Shamrock	Nantwich, Union Inn	12.30 pm
Regulator	Leeds	12.45 pm
Union	Liverpool, Crown Inn	1.45 pm
Balloon	Liverpool, Golden Lion	3.45 pm
Volunteer	Liverpool, Saracen's Head.	5.30 pm
Umpire	Lancaster, Royal Oak	2.30 pm

Royal Buxton	Buxton, Grove Inn	2.30 pm
Pilot	Northwich, Crown Inn	2.45 pm
Independent Potter	Potteries, Castle Hotel	2.45 pm
Independent	London, Golden Cross, Charing Cross	2.45 pm
Telegraph	London, Bull & Mouth	3.45 pm
Herald	London, Spread Eagle, Gracechurch St.	6.45 pm
Rocket	Birmingham, Albion Hotel	2.45 pm
Macclesfield	Macclesfield, Bull's Head.	4.15 pm
Comet	Blackburn, Bull's Head	4.45 pm
Duke of Manchester	Leeds	5.00 pm
Accommodation	Bolton, Ship Inn	5.30 pm

A typical coach was the *Champion* that ran between the Moseley Arms and the Castle and Falcon at Newark. The 76 miles involved 12 changes of horses. Each team covered six miles in just under an hour. On the return journey, the *Champion* left Newark at 5 am and arrived at 4 pm; a run of eleven hours. [66] The excitement and bustle of a coach departure from the top of Market Street was depicted by Mrs Banks. [67]

The open space in front was enlivened by the newly painted London Stage Coach, the Lord Nelson, the fresh scarlet coats of the coachmen and guards, the assembling of the passengers and luggage, the shouting and swearing of the half-wake ost-lers and porters, the grumbling of the first comers (shivering in the raw air) at the unpunctuality of the stages, the excuses of the booking clerk, the self gratulations of the last arrival that he was "in time", the dragging of trunks and portmanteaus onto the top, the thrusting of bags and boxes into the boot, the harnessing of the snorting steeds, the horsing of the vehicle, the scrambling of the outsiders on to the top by ladder and wheel, the self satisfied settlement of the "inside" in the places they had "booked for", the crushing and thrusting of friends with last messages and parting words, the crack of the whip, the sound of the bugle, the prancing of horses, the rattling of wheels and the dashing off up Market Street Lane of the gallant four-in-hand amid the hurrahs of excited spectators.

Slugg, who lived on Market Street found the arrival of the mail coaches a fine sight:

To see a London coach start or arrive afforded me intense pleasure. The mail coaches were invariably painted dark red and black, and each had four horses and both coachman and guard, the latter being dressed in a red coat and a hat having a broad gilt hat band, and he generally wore top boots. There was only one seat behind, which the guard occupied; he was generally provided with a brace of pistols placed within reach. His horn was always a plain long tin one, which sounded but one note and its octave, but in the open country could be heard a great distance. It was blown to give the horse keepers notice to be ready to change horses and to arouse in the night the keepers of the toll bars who were generally quick eared and had the gate open when the mail arrived.

He continues;

There were generally five coachmen and one guard to a London coach. The coachmen used to drive one coach about forty miles and another in on the same day, whilst the guard went through. He used, for instance, to leave Manchester on a Monday, arrive in London on a Tuesday, leave there on Wednesday, arrive here again on Thursday, rest on Friday and start again on Saturday. The usual fees for a journey to London were a shilling to each coachman and half a crown or five shillings to the guard. I have seen the London mail coming at full speed down Piccadilly, whilst I have heard the horn of the guard of the York mail as it came down Oldham Street; then the Birmingham mail, which came down Oxford Road, turning out of Mosley Street; whilst the Liverpool mail, which had deposited its bags at the Post Office, behind the Exchange, as it came up Market Street; all arriving at nearly the same time.[68]

I have found three references to guests at the Moseley Arms in these years. In February 1818, a lawyer dealing with the Astley estate in Dukinfield stayed for five days. He lived well on breakfasts, dinners, teas and suppers, plus wines and newspapers, for a total of £6 6s.

The handwriting on the bill is that of the early entries in the family Bible and is probably Margaret's. Another guest in September 1818 was Anne Lister of Shibden Hall, Halifax. She returned in November, when she found the food better than at the more "genteel" Albion Hotel. "Stopped at the Mosley Arms," she wrote in her diary on the 18th, "at *2 ¼* (i.e. a quarter past two) and got my boots cleaned. Had a thorough washing and brushing..." She noted the *Defiance* coach standing at the door. She did not comment on the Moseley Arms when she visited in 1821 but finally preferred the Bridgewater Arms.[69]

A sad incident in 1821 concerned a certain Henry Scott, tea dealer of Smithfield, who cut his throat at the inn. The chambermaid saw the poor fellow behaving oddly and the waiter, George Howarth, found his door locked when he tried to rouse him. He and a colleague, William Chappell, then looked through the window from the outside and beheld the dreadful scene. Old John later gave the man's personal effects to his friends.[70]

As John prospered, his girls probably spent less time working and more in polishing their persons and manners. If their brother could be a *gentleman*, why should not they be *ladies*? In 1825 Alice was 25, Betsey 22, Margaret 18, Mary 15 and Ann 12. They may have attended Mrs Broadbent's ridiculous school for young ladies in Shudehill, mocked by Mrs Banks. There can be no doubt they flirted with the guests, three of them successfully so. In May 1825, Alice married Robert Bent and a year later, Betsey married William Barnfield, "merchant of the city of London." Both girls received a £300 dowry.[71] These sisters were close and later neighbours in London.

I suspect that Barnfield and Bent, both Londoners, were friends. Robert Bent, aged 24 in 1826, was a book-seller in St Anne's Place, Manchester, but known to the publishing world as the son of William Bent of Paternoster Row, in the city of London.[72] William Bent had founded two book trade magazines in the late 1700s; *The London Catalogue of Books* and the *Monthly Literary Advertiser*.[73] Robert's first partner in Manchester was Samuel Robinson, followed by Robert Robinson in 1824.[74] In that year they had a dispute with their bookbinders who "blacked" of one their fellows. The dispute throws a light on the problems faced by early trade unions trying to assert discipline over members.

> *... a fortnight ago the journeymen bookbinders of Messrs Robinson and Bent of this town threatened their masters with an immediate desertion from their employ, unless they would consent to discharge a valuable servant, who had incurred the displeasure of his comrades by refusing to pay a trivial fine which they had imposed upon him.*[75]

Slugg considered Robinson, whose wife was related to Sir Benjamin Heywood, as a "highly respectable bookseller".[76] In that year, William Bent died and Robert decided to take over the London business, but remained in Manchester for another two years. In 1825, Bent and Robinson published a book of sermons by Alexander Cruden and a certain John Richardson, probably our Old John, was a subscriber.[77] They also donated two books to the library of the Mechanics Institute; *Culpepper's Herbal* and *Barclay's English Dictionary*.[78]

After their marriage, Robert and Alice went to live at 241, Oxford Road, "nearly opposite Rusholme Lane" from where they sold up and left for London in 1827. The auction sale list suggests they were comfortable.

> *Sale of household goods: ... on Friday, 22ⁿᵈ June at 11 o'clock precisely: The remaining part of the HOUSEHOLD FURNITURE, a dinner service of Coalbrookdale Semi-China, a handsome set of Breakfast, Coffee and Tea China, and other effects of Mr Robert Bent who is leaving Manchester – The furniture consists of a set of excellent modern mahogany chairs, a pair of handsome ditto card tables, a ditto Pembroke table, Brussels parlour and stair carpets, a handsome chimney glass, in one plate in a gilt frame, fenders and fire irons, a useful camp bed-stead and bedding, painted wardrobe, chests of drawers, dressing tables, wash-stands and chairs, dressing glasses, some articles of cut glass, a Grecian lobby lamp, the kitchen requisites and other useful articles. – To be viewed on Thursday 21ˢᵗ and on the morning of sale, when catalogues may be had.*[79]

Once in London, Robert inserted the word *Bent's* into the title of the *Literary Advertiser* and the *London Catalogue* and they have remained major sources of information on the London book trade in the 19th century. The Bents went on to have four daughters and a son;[80] their first child, Betsey Richardson Bent, was born at Manchester in 1827.[81] Margaret Jane was born two years later in Middlesex.[82] Both were christened at St John's, Deansgate, in August 1830 when Robert had become a "gentleman," not just a bookseller.[83]

The Barnfield family into which Betsey married were merchants in London and Calcutta. These India merchants, contemptuously called "nabobs," were unpopular in England for flashing their new wealth, but the gentry were happy to marry their daughters. The Barnfields seem to have travelled much between the two countries, but the records do not always distinguish William Barnfield junior from William senior who went to Calcutta in the 1780s.[84] Young William was probably born there in 1801.[85] In 1803, a certain "Master Barnfield" returned to London aboard the *Sovereign* unaccompanied by his parents.[86] It seems he was reared in England. In 1821, Wm. Barnfield junior paid £354 for a bond to export fire-arms to India, with his father, William, of Middleton Terrace, Pentonville, standing surety. He then paid another £500 for the right of residency in India.[87] William's mother was probably the "lady of W. Barnfield of Calcutta" who died at sea aboard the *Circassian* in 1825, aged 52, on her way to England.[88] After their marriage, William and Betsey lived in London where William carried on a wine and spirits business at 17, Mark Lane.[89]

The handwriting in the family Bible suggests that Margaret made certain entries in the summer of 1826. She noted Betsey's and Alice's marriages and left spaces for the marriage details of her other children, but died on the last day of September, aged 54. There is little the old records tell about her, but she was surely a good wife who helped to make John's business succeed. Her burial at Chorley suggests she wished to lie with her late son in her home village.[90]

John, now in his sixtieth year, was left with James, 21, and the unmarried girls, Margaret 18, Mary 16, and Ann 13. Later evidence suggests that James, though modestly competent, was not as energetic as his father, nor perhaps always reliable, and so the family's future remained John's concern. Young Gentleman John was now a family man probably living in pleasant Chorlton on Medlock where he spent most of his adult life. His elder daughter, Mary, was born in 1821 and the younger, Elizabeth, in 1822. A son, John Hardcastle Richardson, followed in 1826.[91] John was making a living as a solicitor, but office drudgery did not suit one who preferred the company of horsey gentry to failed shop-keepers. In those years, a John Richardson, "solicitor," held a series of creditors' meeting at the Moseley Arms, but there were two others of his name practising in the town; one with offices at 27, Princess Street, and one in St James Square.[92] But "Gentleman" John was biding his time, looking to the day when he would become master of the Moseley Arms, a genial mine host, smartly dressed, chatting with his guests and giving orders to those who actually did the work.

PROSPERITY WITH A QUARREL

Widening Market Street – Old John's re-marriage – Young John's career – Piccadilly – The Hotel – Manchester visitors – John's will – The quarrel – John's death – Change at the Moseley Arms.

Gentleman John might dream of becoming the master of the Moseley Arms but his father had no intention of risking the family's future by letting him run the business. It was a time of great change and just as the Royal Oak at Chorley had not generated the income necessary for his ambitions in 1813, neither would the Moseley Arms in the 1820s, so long as it remained cramped into a narrow old lane of rickety buildings. But then the town authorities began to widen Market Street by demolishing the old buildings and replacing them with the edifices of a modern city. John took advantage of this development to transfer to Piccadilly, where his "inn" would become a "hotel." The "Gentleman" could not be allowed to spoil this venture and inevitably there were some sharp words between them, particularly as father had reservations about James, who was only 22 in 1827.

Matters came to a head in 1828 when Old John solved the dilemma by turning to a reliable woman. On January 12th, at the age of 62, he married Mary Withnell, "spinster of this parish and town, at the Collegiate Church.[93] Her surname is that of the parish neighbouring Chorley and she was probably a faithful family servant. She certainly knew how to run the business.

Within days of the marriage, the Gentleman held the last of his creditors' meetings at the Moseley Arms and threw up his legal practice.[94] In a fit of pique, or perhaps as part of a long nourished "Plan B", he made an immediate career change. Gregarious, fun-loving and longing for the open road, he became a "gentleman coachman" of the newest Manchester – London stage-coach, the *Peveril of the Peak*.[95] His great grand-daughter believed he had been a stage-coach driver, but I could never square this with his obsession with his gentlemanly status.[96] Then, after finding John mentioned in a newspaper as "ex-premier of the *Peveril of the Peak*" I learned of "gentlemen coachmen" [97]

These coaching *gentlemen* were often true gentry, even aristocrats like Lord Onslow, the Earl of Barrymore, the 7th Duke of Beaufort and Sir Vincent Cotton, all of whom regularly drove the London coaches. They formed exclusive "driving clubs" and were great swells.[98] Slugg stressed that the *Peveril's* coachmen were "most respectable men," like Labrey from a family of tea dealers, and Watmough, the son of a guards' officer, who had himself been commissioned in the *Scots Greys*.[99] Gentleman John had almost certainly learned to drive at Chorley and if there was some loss of status in becoming a coachman, he kept his commissioner for oaths warrant as proof of his rank.

Meanwhile, old John was busy with the move to Piccadilly. In 1829, the freehold of the Market Street Inn was put up for auction, the newspaper referring to it as "situated in Market Street and Fountain Street … with stables, coach houses, gig houses, warehouses and other apurtenancies in the occupation of Mr John Richardson and Mrs Marple." [100] Then he took over two large houses on the north side of Piccadilly, one the former home of a Mrs Podmore, a famous beauty and the other belonging to James Whitehead, a wealthy bleacher.[101] Piccadilly, formerly known as Levers Row, connected Deansgate to the London Road at Ardwick. The name change was another sign of the Manchester inferiority complex that saw other southern names applied to its thoroughfares, like Oxford, Cambridge and Portland. There was even a Pall Mall.[102] The new Moseley Arms Hotel was at 13, Piccadilly, between Tib Street and Oldham Street and fronting Moseley Street and the west end of the Infirmary garden. It comprised a three-storey building with six tall windows per floor.[103] The frontage was 20 yards and 23 inches and the site covered "898 superficial yards of land, or thereabouts".[104] John announced his move in *The Manchester Courier* on January 16th 1830.

*John Richardson begs respectfully to announce to his numer-
ous Friends and the Public in general, that he has engaged an
extensive range of buildings in Piccadilly, between the White
Bear and Oldham Street, which is now fitting up for his use,
and will, by the time he quits the Moseley Arms, be open for
the reception for such of his Friends as may favour him with a
share of their countenance and support.*

*   J. Richardson avails himself of the present opportunity of
returning his most sincere thanks for the uniform kindness
shown to him by those gentlemen who have for so long a period
given a preference to his house, and assures them that no consideration will influence him to relax in his attention and exertions to promote the comforts of those who may become his
guests – This removal is in consequence of the old Moseley
Arms being about to be converted into warehouses: he cannot
but feel great satisfaction in having had the opportunity of
fixing himself in a situation incomparably more pleasant and
airy, and for all purposes of business unexceptionable.*

The furniture and fittings of the Market Street inn were auctioned off
in March.[105] The move of a hundred yards seems to have been regarded
as a great improvement. "Residence in Piccadilly was pleasant in the
early part of the last century," wrote Swindells.[106]

In 1835, a German visitor who came in from the Stockport road
recorded:

*Entering the town one passes a lovely grassy expanse with
a pond (Ardwick Green) and towards the centre of the town
one is confronted with an attractive, large Infirmary building
which also has a sizeable pond at its front. This (Piccadilly) is
the most beautiful part of the town. Here are also situated the
two largest hotels, the Albion Hotel and the Moseley Arms.*[107]

But Manchester as a whole presented a frightful spectacle to the
French political writer, de Toqueville, in the 1830s.[108]

*A sort of black smoke covers the city. The sun seen through it is
a disc without rays. Under this half-daylight 300,000 human*

beings are ceaselessly at work. A thousand noises disturb this dark labyrinth. From this drain the greatest stream of human industry flows out to fertilise the whole world, from this filthy sewer pure gold flows.

The family's next-door neighbour at the White Bear Hotel was Ben Oldfield, a great character, famous for his poetry, rough humour and practical jokes. He was first an agent for Pickford's, the transport company that supplied horses to the King during the Civil War. But while John concentrated on making the Moseley Arms a centre for stage coach travel, Ben made his establishment one for entertainment. A specimen of his quick wit was noted by Swindells. Ben introduced to a friend a man named Ben Hime with the words, "This is Ben Hime and I'm Ben." He composed several popular songs, "Old England," "Eccles Wakes" and "Manchester's Improving Daily." He was also involved in a premature scheme to make a ship canal from Manchester to the mouth of the Dee. When he died in April 1841; his obiturist concluded that he would have made a name in literature, had he been well educated.[109]

The next few years must have passed well enough. Gentleman John was back in his element on the open road and the rest of the family were enjoying the new hotel. But Old John was becoming unwell, for he (or whoever it was) ceased to serve the Court Leet in 1831 and in August 1832, at the age of 66, he made his will. There were still three unmarried daughters so he put the business in the hands of his new wife, Mary, and son James, in that order. They were made trustees of the estate, along with John Stewart and Richard Smith, and required to run the hotel and its stables for as long as was convenient. Then they were to sell up and divide the proceeds equally among the children. Gentleman John, Betsey Barnfield and Alice Bent were to have their previous gifts deducted from their shares. The right of governorship of the Royal Manchester Institution went to James. Gentleman John was firmly excluded from any role. Mary and James felt they were not sufficiently rewarded for their responsibilities and asked for a better provision and Gentleman John was furious. A frightful row ensued in which the Gentleman roused a commotion about the hotel.

In reply, Old John amended his will to allow James and Mary £100 per year, "until the youngest of my children attain the age of twenty one years" and dealt with young John in a codicil.

> *And I do hereby further order and direct and wish it to be taken as part of my Will that my son John Richardson shall not directly or indirectly interfere or meddle in my said trade or business of in the Trusts of my said Will or Codicil And I do hereby further direct that in case my said son John shall cause or create any disturbance in or about the same or with any part of my Family on account thereof the share or interest of my property which I have in and by my said Will given to him shall go to and be divided unto and equally between and amongst my other children share and share alike.*

This placed the young John's interest in the Moseley Arms in peril. He must not "interfere or meddle" or "cause or create any disturbance" and the executors would be the judge and jury of the matter.

On May 1st 1833, Cumberland John died and was buried at Chorley.[110] He was very much a child of his times, though one of the more successful. From the Wigton poorhouse he had made good. Somehow he became a successful businessman, a worthy citizen of Manchester and, in a small way, a patron of the arts. He left Cumberland when men remembered the passing of Bonnie Prince Charlie, lived through the age of the French Revolution and died well-off in a city in the Age of Steam. There can be little doubt that he was a hard man, but withal a humane one. The fact that Richard Hough approved of him and that he treasured Hurd's *Religions of the World*, and probably subscribed to Cruden's *Sermon*s, suggests that he was a conventionally good-living man.

After the funeral, the Gentleman may have flown into a rage, interfered, meddled or caused a disturbance; or he may merely have expressed his disgust at his father's arrangements. But on May 28th, the executors enforced the sanction prescribed in the codicil and he was disinherited.[111] There is another hint that the changeover at the Moseley Arms was not without snags, particularly with regard to the coach office. Mary and James placed a notice in the *Worcester Herald* on October 26th. Similar notices did not appear in other newspapers so it may have addressed rumours, perhaps hatched by Gentleman John, circulating in a town where important customers lived.[112]

Moseley Arms Hotel, Piccadilly, Manchester,

MARY AND JAMES RICHARDSON

Trustees of the late John Richardson

In returning their most grateful acknowledgements to the Gentry, Commercial Gentlemen and others for the past patronage beg to inform them the business will, in future, be carried on by them and they earnestly solicit a continuance of their kind support.

M and J also take this opportunity of stating that a GENERAL COACH OFFICE is now open, where coaches to all parts of the Country go direct from the house.

Manchester. October 1833

The enforcement of the codicil disinherited Gentleman John's heirs, so there was no truth behind the belief later cherished by his daughter Mary Jane (Polly) and passed down to my father's generation, that his children ought to have shared in the winding up of the Moseley Arms. The consequences for certain of Cumberland John's great-grandchildren were dire. Later in the century, as they toiled in cotton mills for miserable wages, they dreamed of what might have been. His more fortunate descendants who were born into wealthy families probably never knew of his existence.

THE LIFE OF A COACHMAN
AND THE DEATH OF A DIVA

*Gentleman coachmen of Manchester – The Peveril of the Peak
– A bachelor again – Robert Lodge – Bent family's woes –
Barnfield family's woes – Death of Maria Malibran.*

After Cumberland John died, Gentleman John became estranged
from his brother, sisters and step-mother. They continued to live at
the Moseley Arms Hotel whilst he and his family lived elsewhere.
His coaching duties must have taken him away from home, even if
he covered only the *Peveril*'s stages nearest to Manchester. There can
be little doubt he was now in his preferred element, swaggering about
inn yards in top boots and great coat and brandishing a great whip. He
was probably friendly with Robert Bradbury between 1828 and the
latter's death in 1831 and probably shared the *Peveril's* "box" with
him on occasion. Stage-coach drivers were themselves regarded as
celebrities, and their skills were admired for good reason; a loaded,
top-heavy, three-ton coach with primitive brakes rattling along at 15
to 20 miles an hour needed careful handling. One going at full tilt
was an almost fearsome spectacle. Serious accidents were common,
and unlike with a car crash, when everything stops after the impact,
an upturned coach would be dragged along on its side by injured
and terrified horses in a frightful tangle of harness, shattered wheels,
broken axles and mangled bodies. Hence, the whole aura of stage-
coach travel was romantic, as the literature of the time reveals. A
passage in *Tom Brown's Schooldays* tells of Tom's journey across East
Anglia on a winter's night and shows that coach travel often meant
hurried suppers, gulped ale, black roads, biting winds and rain. Tom's
coach was the *Tally-Ho,* "a tip-top goer – ten miles an hour, including
stoppages, and so punctual that all the road set their clocks by her."

A publication of 1827 describes the typical coachman.[113]

He has commonly a broad, full face, curiously mottled with red, as if the blood had been forced by hard feeding into every vessel of the skin; he is swelled into jolly dimensions by frequent potations of malt liquors, and his bulk is still further increased by a multiplicity of coats, in which he is buried like a cauliflower, the upper one reaching to his heels. He wears a broad-brimmed low-crowned hat, a huge roll of coloured handkerchief about his neck, knowingly knotted and tucked in at the bosom; and has in summer time a large bouquet of flowers in his button-hole; the present, most probably, of some enamoured country lass. His waistcoat is commonly of some bright colour, striped, and his smallclothes extend far below the knees, to meet a pair of jockey boots which reach about half way up his legs.

All this costume is maintained with much precision; he has a pride of having his clothes of excellent materials; and, notwithstanding the seeming grossness of his appearance, there is still discernible that neatness and propriety of person, which is almost inherent in an Englishman. He enjoys great consequence and consideration along the road; has frequent conferences with the village housewives, who look upon him as a man of great trust and dependence; and he seems to have a good understanding with every bright-eyed country lass. The moment he arrives where the horses are to be changed, he throws down the reins with something of an air, and abandons the cattle to the care of the hostler; his duty being merely to drive them from one stage to another. When, off the box, his hands are thrust in the pockets of his great coat, and he rolls about the inn yard with an air of the most absolute lordliness. Here he is generally surrounded by an admiring throng of hostlers, stable-boys, shoe-blacks, and those nameless hangers-on, that infest inns and taverns, and run errands, and do all kind of odd jobs, for the privilege of battening on the drippings of the kitchen and the leakage of the tap-room.

*These all look up to him as to an oracle; treasure up his cant
phrases; echo his opinions about horses and other topics of
jockey lore; and, above all, endeavour to imitate his air and
carriage. Every ragamuffin that has a coat to his back, thrusts
his hands in the pockets, rolls in his gait, talks slang, and is
an embryo Coachey.*

The *Peveril of the Peak,* named after the eponymous hero of Sir
Walter Scott's 1823 novel, was started in 1828 by John Knowles
of the *Peacock*, Market Street. Strictly speaking we should refer to
the "service" rather than the "coach," since several vehicles were
in use at any one time. A daily two-way service required at least
two coaches; say four in total with back-ups. Each journey needed
three coachmen and one guard – so some 10 to 20 coachmen were
employed at any one time. The *Peveril* first ran with two horses, but
later had six magnificent piebalds. It ran along the route that became
the A6; via Stockport, Disley, Buxton, Bakewell, Matlock, Derby,
Loughborough, Leicester, Kettering and Bedford, and at its best did
the run in 17 hours. Knowles reduced the five coachmen to three and
for a long time it was the fastest coach on the road.[114] In 1828, with
two horses, it left London an hour after the mail coach but delivered
the Bakewell post half an hour earlier and reached Manchester in 23
hours.[115] In that year, Richard Cobden, the anti-Corn Law campaigner,
made the journey in the "marvellously short space of 20 hours." [116]
On May Day 1829, the *Peveril* was at Manchester "drawn by 6 beautiful piebald horses, richly caparisoned" [117] and in June 1830, built
"on a new construction", it was at Buxton, drawn by six fine piebalds
in "exceedingly fine trappings." [118] An American visitor in 1832,
described the *Peveril* as "admirably managed and horsed." [119] Slugg
mentions a journey he made by the *Peveril* in its first year.

*The Peveril of the Peak used to attract a good deal of attention
on account of four handsome piebald horses attached to it as
it left the Peacock at noon. In the midsummer of 1828 I paid
a visit with my mother to some relatives near Dunstable, and
we returned to Lancashire by the Peveril of the Peak, which
was then only a pair-horsed coach. We joined it a place called*

Market Street, near Dunstable, at about 10 o'clock p.m. I well remember the night was wet, and the inside of the coach being full, my mother was obliged to travel outside, and sat next to the driver. Being then only a two-horsed coach it had no guard, and I sat behind.

At some small town through which we passed, about three or four o'clock in the morning, we changed horses and had a horse put in which backed the coach against a garden wall. It was a beautiful morning and I had a lady companion who was charmed with the beauties of the sky; whilst I, timid lad, was full of fears as to the safety of the coach. However, we got off all right, and came to Manchester through Derby, Matlock, and Buxton – a magnificent drive – and we arrived about four o'clock.[120]

But the *Peveril* had its share of accidents. In March 1830, it ran over two boys at Heaton Norris, killing one. The passengers signed a statement swearing to the driver's sobriety and good conduct, and that the boys had run into the horses when chasing a hoop.[121] There were another nine serious accidents over the next six years. In June 1831, the coach overturned at Kettering, breaking the coachman's leg.[122] There was another very nasty incident in December near Derby, when an un-manned and heavily laden Pickford's van ran into the *Peveril*, killing the coachman, John Arkwright. The van's drivers had gone to the pub, leaving the team in charge of boys who had allowed them take off.[123] In 1835, James Pollard painted the *Peveril* outside the Peacock, Islington, revealing that it sported the star and garter motif.[124] In that year it collided with a cart between Derby and Shardlow, killing a lady passenger, and in October it ran over Samuel Cross, a Greenwich pensioner, in Holloway; no blame attaching to the coachman.[125]

Our John must have had some near misses. Was he, perhaps, the *Peveril* coachman fined £2-10s and 10s costs for dodging the toll at Shardlow in 1830.[126] Or the one fined for "furious driving" at Loughborough in 1834? [127] Was he ever robbed, like his colleague, Grosvenor, who was relieved of 5 shillings by two highway men at

Mountsorrel in 1831? [128] Was he the awful rotter whose conduct was recounted by an anonymous writer in the *Dublin University Magazine* in 1842?

> *I remember once coming into Matlock on top of the Peveril of the Peak" he wrote, "when the coachman, who drove four spanking thoroughbreds, contrived in something less than five minutes, to excite his whole team to the very top of their temper, lifting the wheelers almost off the ground with his heavy lash and thrashing the leaders till they smoked with passion, he brought them up to the inn door, trembling with rage and snorting with anger. What the devil is all this for, thought I. He guessed at once what was passing in my mind, and, with a knowing touch of his elbow, whispered 'There's a new coachman going to try 'em out, and I'll leave him a precious legacy'.* [129]

Ominously, this last phrase might have come readily to a solicitor. In 1835, John was living with his family on Chester Street, Chorlton upon Medlock, a suburb then filling up with new middle-class housing.[130] His income from fees, tips and perhaps investments would have been enough to keep him "respectable." Apparently the coach driver collected a shilling from each passenger, so a full coach would yield ten to twelve shillings for each journey.[131] He may have invested in the coach business, when the future belonged to the railways.

But in 1835, Elizabeth, his wife, died at the age of 34 and was interred in the Hardcastle vault at St John's, Deansgate.[132] This suggests that John was not up to buying his own plot. He was left with three children, Mary 14, Elizabeth 12, and John 9 and could not cope. So the children went to live with their maternal grandmother, Grace, who was remarried to a wealthy Scottish estate agent, James Chambers, and living in Pool Street, now the western edge of Albert Square.[133]

John then returned to a bachelor life. At the census of 1841, he asserted that he was "a gentleman of independent means;" not a coachman working for wages. He shared a house in nearby Chatham Street with a young gentleman named Robert Lodge and a servant girl.[134]

He may have been Lodge's guest or, more likely, given the 18-year age difference, Lodge's landlord. Robert was a Yorkshire man in the dyestuffs trade and later a partner with W. H. Watkins, whose daughter he married. His business was in Indian indigo, but the advent of aniline dyes ended it, so in the 1860s after he had quickly lost his wife and three young daughters, he sold out and returned to his native Bishopdale where he increased his family estates and became a gentleman farmer at the Rookery, a Victorian Gothic hall graced with landscaped gardens. He bred pedigree shorthorn cattle, once selling a bull for £2,000. He died, aged 72, in 1888. His son became colonel of the 3rd Garrison, Yorkshire Regiment. [135] These were the sort of people Gentleman John liked to associate with.

For several years, the *Peveril* left the Peacock on Market Street at half past noon. John would perhaps have strolled from home along Mosley Street and taken an early lunch. Then he would examine, with an expert eye, the six piebalds as they stamped and impatiently rattled their bits. He would then address the passengers before an admiring throng, mount the box and taking up the reins, call out, "Stand clear." Then they would set off at a merry trot along Piccadilly into London Road. In the summertime the ride out would be very pleasant. Beyond Ardwick Green, the road cut across open country through, Longsight and Levenshulme to Stockport. Then on to Bullock Smithy, now called Hazel Grove, where the cobbled turnpike ended. [136] Then the slow climb through High Lane to the Ram's Head at Disley where the horses were changed for the longer run up to Buxton. John Critchley Prince, the Hyde poet, described the sensation of passing into Derbyshire.

> *In the month of July 1830 ... I took a place on the Peveril of the Peak stage coach bound for London ... I was delighted as we passed into Derbyshire. I became absorbed in the ever-changing panorama of mountains, vales and river which characterises that romantic country. The bare and breezy heights of Buxton, the rude and rocky passes beyond, and above all, that paradise of valleys – Matlock, wound me up to a pitch of silent enthusiasm and it was not until we got into the flat coun-*

try that my mind came down to the level of everyday things.[137]

At Matlock, John would hand the coach over to another driver and spend a merry evening at the inn. Next day the return trip would bring him home. Such a life offered plenty of scope for boozing, flirting and gambling, had he been so inclined. But it would be unpleasant work in bad weather. In late December 1836, the *Peveril,* perhaps under John's charge, was abandoned in a snowdrift somewhere in Derbyshire, to the great satisfaction of those on the *Bruce* which passed it by.[138]

Back in Manchester, I guess John frequented his old haunts with his old cronies. Almost certainly he knew Knowles's son, John, who took over the *Theatre Royal* and continued with pantomimes in the Robert Bradbury tradition. But the spectacle of their father re-living his youth seems to have distressed John's daughters; though James and Grace Chambers took a more tolerant view. John probably paid for their upkeep but otherwise neglected them. At some point in these years he had his portrait painted in oils.[139]

Meanwhile in London, Robert Bent's publishing venture was flourishing, with the sales of the *Advertiser* reaching 1165 in 1835.[140] In 1831, Alice produced a son who was named after his uncle, William Barnfield Bent.[141] In March 1834, when the family lived on Upper Stamford Street, Lambeth, London, their two-year old daughter, Mary Elizabeth, died and another child, Marianne, was born.[142] Then, on August 30th, Alice died "after a few hours illness." [143] The tragedy affected Robert badly and thereafter he seems to have struggled. In 1839, he dissolved his partnership with David Kidd in the *Advertiser,*[144] though it continued with the *Bent* name in the title, and in 1842 he sold the *Catalogue* to Thomas Hodgson who ran it until 1860.[145] He remained a book-seller and stationer at Aldine Chambers, Paternoster Row, but like Gentleman John, found it impossible to bring up children without a wife. His daughters therefore came up to Manchester to be brought up at the Moseley Arms by Uncle James and his sisters.[146] However, at the 1841 census, the two elder girls, Betsey, aged 15 and Margaret, ten, were in London at the house of a musician who ran a school in Upper Stamford Street. When they grew up they regarded the Moseley Arms as their home, though Robert's son stayed in London and followed his father in the book and stationery business.

The Barnfields were Robert's neighbours on Upper Stamford Street.[147] However, William, fell into a financial scrape and over the next ten years struggled to pay off his creditors. *Perry's Bankrupt Gazette* and the London newspapers recorded the prolonged financial agony of W. Barnfied, the Mark Lane wine merchant.[148] In the 1840s, he and Betsey went out to Calcutta and tried their luck again.[149]

After Cumberland John's death in 1833, a number of stage coaches stopped running from the Moseley Arms.[150] But Mary and James continued to attract the best clientele. In May 1834, several local doctors met at the hotel to discuss lobbying Parliament with regard to medical qualifications and then went on to found the Manchester Medical Society.[151] In 1836, the newly established Manchester City Corporation celebrated, with some pomp, its purchase of the ancient manorial rights from Sir Oswald Moseley. On the night of the annual fair, according to an ancient custom, the Reeve declared the event open from the Moseley's steps and then the Mayor and city council members went in for a splendid banquet.[152]

Later in 1836, one of the Moseley's most flamboyant guests briefly made the hotel known throughout the world. Maria Malibran was one of the greatest singers of all time and in September 1825, as the 16 year old Maria Garcia, she had stayed with her family at the old inn on Market Street. They were a colourful Spanish family of opera singers, normally resident in France. The patriarch, Manuel Garcia, born in Seville in 1775, was a master of his profession, but an utter brute; arrogant, violent, jealous, and dogged by rumours that he had escaped the gallows for murder. His mistress and her child accompanied them and they all lived in terror of his rages. However, he taught them to sing well. Maria enjoyed her stay and sang in the town's theatres before her family moved on to Liverpool from whence they sailed for New York.[153]

In the following years Maria gained a worldwide reputation but

Maria Malibran

her personal life was turbulent. Within five months of arriving in America she married a middle-aged French businessman, Eugene Malibran, perhaps from youthful infatuation, but more probably to escape her father, whose dramatic death threats quite terrified her when she sang opposite him in *Othello*. On the other hand her motive might have been entirely mercenary, because when Malibran went broke two years later; she left him and went to France.

She arrived in Paris just at the right moment. The French Romantic movement was blossoming after the repressions of the Revolution and its attendant wars, and artists and writers were eager to exploit their new freedom. Within months, Maria Malibran was a sensation. She brought to the opera a vitality and excitement that quite entranced her audiences. Rossini, Paganini, Bellini, Chopin and a host of others, were captivated. Experts found it hard to define her quality for her voice was not perfect, but she left her audiences emotionally drained. They had never experienced anything quite like it and the world fell in love with her.

She then fell in love with a Belgian violinist, Charles de Beriot, and though both were supposed to be devout Catholics, they overcame the problem of Maria's existing husband by tricking a priest into marrying them. Thereafter, she added "de Beriot" to her name of Maria Malibran. Between 1830 and 1836, she was fully occupied with marriage and career, but her life was not calm. She was vivacious and high spirited, but moody and hysterical. She lived irresponsibly and rode dangerous horses, seeming to emulate in real life the trials and tragedies of her stage characters. Her health suffered and she fell under the spell of an Italian quack, "Dr" Belluomini.

In 1836 Malibran agreed to perform at a great music festival to be held in Manchester in the September, but one morning in early July, in Regent's Park, London, she fell from a frisky horse and suffered severe bruising. Despite the doctor's advice, she would not rest and became morbidly attached to the idea of playing the martyr to her art; a popular theme for the French romantics. But she had been mortally injured. She was pregnant and probably her unborn child died *in utero*. Her health deteriorated steadily.

On the afternoon of Sunday, September 11th 1836, she and de Beriot arrived in Manchester with one servant and booked into the Royal Hotel. But on hearing that some friends, including the Italian singer, Luigi Lablache, were at the Moseley Arms they moved there.[154] Lablache had travelled northwards in the *Peveril of the Peak* coach with other celebrities, Madame Cadori Allan, Mademoiselle Assandri and Ivanoff, and they were all seriously shaken up when the coach overturned. The driver, who was not our John, was trapped under the vehicle for two hours and later died.[155]

On her arrival, Maria told Mary Richardson that she was struck by the co-incidence of being given room number 9 at the Moseley Arms Hotel, just as she had at the old inn. Mary pointed out that had been 12 years before, so Mary must have remembered that previous visit, which supports the notion she had been a family servant.[156] Then with their newly arrived friends, the Beriots passed a pleasant evening of light-hearted merriment round the piano. Mary was concerned about Malibran's condition since news of her fall and rumours of her resulting lassitude had preceded her. Malibran was not well for two days, and on the Wednesday, vomited after a breakfast of oysters and porter. Mary suggested that perhaps the porter did not agree with her. "What can I do?" she answered, "I must take something for my voice and I find this the best thing I can take."

The Peveril of the Peak at the Peacock Inn, Islington, London
Painted by James Pollard in 1835

Malibran then started on a series of exacting performances while a mood of melodrama began to envelop the scene. The great lady, still only 28 years old, but visibly sick, strained to produce the most exalted music most Mancunians were ever likely to hear. On the Thursday, she returned to the hotel exhausted and complained to Mary of pains in the head. Beriot, though attentive, was gloomy and apathetic.

In fact, he was practically useless and Malibran turned to Mary for support. By Friday the 16th, she was very ill and Mary advised her to rest. But she would not. "I have been trying my voice in bed," she replied, "and it is as strong and clear, and I have as much power as though I were in perfect health." Beriot also wished her to stay in bed but she was determined to sing. Mary helped her to dress and attended to her hair, but she vomited again and when the Boroughreeve's coach arrived, she had to be helped into it on her hands and knees. She was then driven to the Collegiate Church, with de Beriot and Mary, to give a performance of sacred music, but on arrival she went into hysterics, her shrieks echoing through the ancient rafters to the astonishment of the onlookers. The party returned to the hotel without her having sung a note. Beriot had his own concert that night, so Mary sat up with Maria. The two must have got into confidences, because Malibran told Mary that she had known Beriot for nine years and had been married for seven, but could only let the knowledge become public for the last two. She had been "blest," she told Mary, "with a most affectionate husband."

Malibran continued unwell the next day. The doctors thought she would recover but, in despair, Beriot wrote to Belluomini in London, begging him to come at once. The quack left immediately by post chaise and arrived at the Moseley Arms at 6.30 pm on the 18th. Malibran was delighted and was certain he could save her. There followed some professional animosity between the medical men, but Belluomini's potions reduced Malibran's fever and she felt a little better the next day. But on the 22nd she deteriorated and Belluomini, fearing the unborn child was dead, called for a second opinion. Mary suggested Mr Lewis, a local obstetrician. Lewis looked briefly at the patient and said the child was probably dead and the mother would soon follow. From then on Malibran faded away. At twenty-five to midnight on Friday, 23rd September, attended by Mary and Belluomini, she died.

Mary informed Beriot who lay in a stupor in the next room. To her amazement, he proposed, under Belluomini's promptings, to leave for London at once. He wrote a brief letter to the Festival Committee, authorising them to organise the burial and then fell into a daze. Mary and his manservant packed his belongings and helped him out of the hotel to join Belluomini in the carriage. Deeply touched by Mary's kindness, he gave her Malibran's ring, a turquoise set in black enamel, and a locket containing a tress of her hair. Then, at half past one in the morning, the coach rattled away down Piccadilly.

When the news broke next morning, the public reacted with the morbid hysteria seen at the death of Diana, Princess of Wales, 160 years later. The tragedy bore the mark of the gods; a divine creature was called to Olympus. And as with the princess's death, souvenir hunters and hungry newspaper reporters descended on the scene. Mary drove them all away but the reporters bribed some of the hotel servants and were allowed to glimpse the corpse. Mary later refused lucrative offers for mementos, including one of ten guineas for one of La Malibran's slippers. However, the spurned reporters got their revenge by inventing and publishing spiteful rumours about Mary.

The whole business now took a curious turn that led to recriminations that lasted years. Mancunians were shocked when de Beriot did not return for the funeral. Instead he left for Brussels, almost certainly because their marriage was not legally valid and Malibran's money might fall into the wrong hands. Dr Belluomini wrote a lying letter to Mary testifying that de Beriot could not return to Manchester because he was spitting blood.[157] The Festival Committee then went ahead with a grand funeral on October 1st.The Roman Catholic service for the dead was held at the hotel before the cortege lead off to the Collegiate Church where a Catholic family tomb had been opened. The procession of carriages reached up Piccadilly and down Lever Street, while silent crowds lined the route. In the leading carriages were the chief mourners, the Earl of Wilton, Sir George Smart, Alfred Bunn (a London impresario), the civic dignitaries and Mary Richardson.

Manchester felt it had acquitted itself well in honouring the great lady, despite the unseemly behaviour of her husband, so there was outrage when de Beriot let it be known that he wanted Maria's body exhumed from a Protestant church and re-interred in holy Catholic ground in Belgium. He was not above committing perjury to a priest, but this burial was altogether too much for his tender conscience. There followed an ugly uproar in the press, with sectarian malice and slanders flying in all directions. An exhumation for re-interment was not legally straightforward, and not daring to show his face in the town, De Beriot sent his lawyer cousin, Jean Baptiste de Fiennes, to handle the matter. Fiennes bore an ancient aristocratic name and was descended through the Flemish gentry. He arrived at the Moseley Arms in early October and his patient work at the consistory court at Chester eventually led to Malibran's body being removed in a macabre scene enacted in the early hours of December 20th.

> *At a few minutes after 5 o'clock on Tuesday morning, Monsieur Fiennes, accompanied by Mr Lewis, surgeon, Mr Ewart and Mr Barnfield of London, proceeded to the Collegiate Church.*[158]

It looks as if de Fiennes needed moral support and William Barnfield, forgetting his money worries for a moment, rose to the occasion. Maria's mother had come to Manchester and accompanied the hearse back to the Moseley Arms where she took leave of the Richardson family to whom she had become affectionately attached. Eventually, though not without further controversy, Malibran was re-interred at Laeken, near Brussels.

Malibran's death spawned a number of conspiracy theories, particularly in the French press which, among other calumnies, accused the Richardsons of having poisoned her. Belluomini accused the Manchester doctors of incompetence and they accused him of quackery. Mary came in for snide criticism from the nosey journalists whom she had repelled from the hotel. *The Literary Gazette* sniffily reported:

> *The house at which Malibran died at Manchester, has, we are told, become quite a place of resort for the curious, and Mrs Richardson, the landlady, is making a fortune by showing it to visitors, and detailing all the incidents of the fatal catastrophe, illustrated by pointing out the precise spots where they occurred.*[159]

That this was a big lie was shown by April Fitzlyon, Malibran's most thorough biographer. She concluded, "On one thing everyone agreed; Mrs Richardson, the landlady of the Moseley Arms …behaved impeccably throughout and continued to do so after La Malibran's death." The *Manchester Courier*, on November 9th 1836, referred to "the respected landlady of the Moseley Arms."

Jean Baptiste de Fiennes did not spend all his time at the Moseley Arms at his legal work. He eyed Cumberland John's 24-year-old daughter, Ann, and decided she would make him a good wife. Nor did he waste much time in courting. On September 25th 1837, just two days after the first anniversary of Malibran's death, they were married at St. Johns, Deansgate, after which Jean Baptiste signed his name in a florid hand in the family Bible. In July the next year, Ann gave birth to a son who died two months later.[160]

Room 9 at the Moseley Arms became a place of pilgrimage for morbid romantics who revelled in the tragedy that had occurred within its narrow confines. Alfred Bunn, who had been shown the room by Mary when Maria's coffin lay there, wrote that it was "…a very small room lighted by two windows looking out upon a dull wall. In it was a bed of narrow dimensions, and rather mean furniture." But despite its simplicity, folk wanted to sleep there. Franz Liszt, in 1840, was moved to write from room 9, "Poor Malibran… She was an abundant woman (as Victor Hugo said to me one day) who was, perhaps, right to die young."

Thus, for a brief moment, the family stood in the glare of world attention. The light it throws on them is limited but interesting. First, the part played by Mary suggests that James did not take the lead in running the hotel, though this impression may arise from the intimacy between the two women. But it fits with the hint in John's will; that since Mary was to run the business with James, and not *vice versa*, James may not have been always reliable. The second point is that Mary was a capable woman who inspired affection and commanded respect; in short, a worthy consort of Cumberland John.

GENTLEMAN JOHN'S FIRST BROOD

*James Chambers – Gentleman John's daughters – The Peveril
of the Peak's last days – James Chambers' will – John Hall –
Chartists at the Moseley Arms – James Chambers' death.*

John seems to have got on well with James Chambers who proved a
superb guardian of his children. James was born in 1789 in the parish
of St Mungo, Dumfriesshire,[161] and must have arrived in Manchester
as a young man. He married Grace after John Hardcastle's death, in
1804, but since she was 26 years his senior it is unlikely this was
before 1810, when he was 21.[162] In 1813, a certain James Chambers
of Manchester went bankrupt and one wonders whether marriage to
money was James's desperate remedy.[163] On the other hand, it may
have been a love-match for James gave up any prospect of children and
supported his wife's family generously. He could have been a stone
mason at 11, Russell Street, Chorlton on Medlock in 1837, before he
became a successful builders' merchant, property valuer and estate
agent.[164] He took an active interest in Scottish affairs and joined a
committee set up in Manchester to relieve poverty in the Highlands.[165]
In 1843, he joined another committee of Manchester Scots to support
the newly formed Free Church of Scotland. A friend in both activities
was Robert Barbour, a Scots merchant from Renfrewshire who lived
in Portland Place. Swindells wrote of his achievements in amassing a
large fortune and marrying his daughter to Sir Windham Anstruther;
and of his piety in donating £12,000 to the Presbyterian College in
London.[166] He was chairman of the Manchester-Birmingham Railway
Company, [167] and in 1843, laid the foundation stone of Manchester's
Presbyterian Church in Grosvenor Square.[168]

In June 1841, Mary, John's eldest daughter, at the age of 20, married Edward Roberts, the son of Owen Roberts, a neighbouring shop-

keeper in Pool Street. Edward was a warehouseman and the marriage certificate describes John as "gentleman".[169] Mary's later history is clouded in mystery but she went to Cliff, in Yorkshire, where she gave birth to a daughter, Ellen, in 1845.[170] In December 1841, Elizabeth, aged 19, married a talented young silversmith, John Hall, of 56, King Street, but their marriage certificate recorded that John was a solicitor again.[171] James Chambers and his niece, Jessie Chambers, were their witnesses.[172] Elizabeth and Jessie were good friends and Elizabeth named a daughter after her.

So John had stopped coach driving and resumed his old profession. This was almost certainly due to the coming of the railways which reduced gentlemen coachmen to glorified cab-drivers. The opening of the Grand Trunk Railway to Manchester in July 1837 finished the *Royal Mail*, *Bruce* and *Red Rover*.[173] The *Peveril of the Peak* struggled on, but by 1839 it was down to plying the Manchester – Derby route and then the Manchester – Leeds run, being involved in an accident at Oldham.[174] By 1840, it was adapting its times to meet the trains at Derby.[175] John must have been hopelessly rusty at the law after 13 years, but a solicitor's desk was surely more comfortable than the top of a coach on a wet night. He had undoubtedly enjoyed his days on the road, indeed, the "premier" of the *Peveril of the Peak*, as a newspaper described him in 1849.[176] But Slugg, whilst speaking well of the *Peveril's* drivers in general, did not mention him. Did he deliberately exclude him from such company? I very much fear that our John was more the sort of coachman that George Borrow described.

> *The stage-coachmen of England, at the time of which I am speaking, considered themselves mighty fine gentry, nay, I verily believe, the most important personages of the realm, and their entertaining this high opinion of themselves can scarcely be wondered at; they were low fellows, but masters of driving; driving was in fashion, and sprigs of nobility used to dress as coachmen and imitate the slang and behaviour of coachmen, from whom occasionally they would take lessons in driving as they sat beside them on the box, which post of*

honour any sprig of nobility who happened to take a place on a coach claimed as his unquestionable right; and then these sprigs would smoke cigars and drink sherry with the coach-men in bar-rooms, and on the road; and, when bidding them farewell, would give them a guinea or a half-guinea, and shake them by the hand, so that these fellows, being low fel-lows, very naturally thought no small liquor of themselves, but would talk familiarly of their friends lords so and so, the honourable misters so and so, and Sir Harry and Sir Charles, and be wonderfully saucy to any one who was not a lord, or something of the kind; and this high opinion of themselves received daily augmentation from the servile homage paid them by the generality of the untitled male passengers, espe-cially those on the forepart of the coach, who used to contend for the honour of sitting on the box with the coachman when no sprig was nigh to put in his claim.[177]

Borrow welcomed the railways for removing these "gentlemen" forever. Wilkie Collins took another view.

The last stage Coachman! It falls upon the ear of every one but a shareholder in railways, with a boding, melancholy sound ... our hearts grow heavy at the thought of never again beholding the sweet-smelling nosegay, the unimpeachable top boots, and fair white breeches; once so prominent as the uni-form of the fraternity. With all our respect for expeditious and business-like travelling, we experience a feeling nearly akin to disgust, at being marshalled to our places by a bell and a fellow with a badge on his shoulder; instead of hearing the cheery summons 'Now then, gentlemen,' and being regaled by a short and instructive conversation with a ruddy-faced per-sonage in a dustless olive green coat and prismatic belcher handkerchief. What did we want with smoke? Had we not the coachman's cigar...?... Who would be so unreasonable as to languish for steam, when he could inhale it on a cool, autum-nal morning, naturally concocted from the backs of four blood horses? [179]

In 1842, James Chambers drew up two wills; one under English law for his English estate and another under Scots law for his farms in Dumfriesshire. His English estate comprised properties in Hulme and Oxford Road, so, being childless and having made provision for Grace, he divided his estate among his nephews and nieces; and the Richardson children. The will provided for some rather complicated trusts, but they were to yield £670 a year for young John H. Richardson and £335 a year for each of the girls; with provision for their children after their deaths. These were not small amounts. James also required each Richardson child to pay £20 per annum to their grandmother and after her death, the same amount to their father during his life. His friend, Robert Barbour, was named as a trustee.

The bequests to young John Hardcastle Richardson and Gentleman John came with a condition; the money was not to be used as security for loans or to pay off debts, especially in case of bankruptcy. The actual words were, "*If he become bankrupt, or take the benefit of any Act now or hereafter to be in force for the relief of insolvent debtors, or charge or anticipate the same, then his interest shall cease as if he were dead*." This adds to the strong suspicion that Gentleman John had a record of financial incompetence that James Chambers would not overlook; though otherwise well disposed towards him. The condition led to trouble. The executors were a certain Samuel Gratrix, lead merchant, and John Hall, silversmith, young Elizabeth's husband. The will was never drawn up and when the time came, the executors had to rely on the draft.

Our John must have known Samuel Gratrix. In 1819 he was a plumber and glazier at 6, Bridge Street and in 1841, lived in Chorlton on Medlock.[180] Over the years, he branched into brass founding, lead moulding and building supplies. He was a hard-nosed businessman and slum landlord, who was once fined for poor sanitation in his cottages in Ardwick. He pathetically tried to argue that more privies would have caused more disease.[181] On the other hand, he contributed to charities for poor Irish protestant clergymen and for public parks in Manchester.[182] His business was still going in the early 20th century.

John's son-in-law, John Hall, was described as a goldsmith and silversmith "of the very first rank" and became very rich.[183] He was born in 1804 at Bowden, near Altrincham, where his father was a farrier.[184] At the age of 26, and having presumably completed his apprenticeship, he went into partnership with his master, William Hatfield, as a silversmith, watchmaker and jeweller in King Street, Manchester.[185] He was interested in the metals trade and formed another partnership with William Wilson in an ironmongery business, known first as Messrs Hall & Wilson, and then as Messrs John Hall & Co. Between 1848 and 1851 they made carriage clocks at 56, King Street, some now collectors' pieces.[186]

Hall went on to become an industrialist but he was foremost a silversmith. In 1844, he and Hatfield made three splendid silver salvers, bought by public subscription for John Knowles junior, the son of the founder of the *Peveril of the Peak* stage-coach and the proprietor of the *Theatre Royal*. They were presented at a dinner at the Queen's Hotel in 1844, but Gentleman John was not among the guests, perhaps because he had come down in the world.[187] In 1847, Hall made a silver vase presented to Manchester fire brigade's chief officer, William Rose, on his retirement.[188]

> *The testimonial consists of a large silver vase the workmanship of Mr John Hall, silversmith, King Street, richly embossed, and weighing upwards of 130 ounces. On one side is a representation of Phaeton in his chariot, stopped by Neptune; and on the other side is a gorgeously ornamented shield, upon which is wrought the inscription. The vase stands on a plain square pedestal and is supported by three figures of the phoenix having widely extended wings. The interior of the vase is richly gilt, it has a magnificent gilt cover, the workmanship of which is remarkably elegant. This beautiful piece of plate may be used as a fruit or flower stand or as a bowl upon festive occasions; in the last respect its capacity will be great as it will hold about three gallons. The vase is enclosed in an immense glass of about three quarters of a yard in height.*

In 1847, Hall bought farmland near Lancaster with James Hall, probably his brother, of Bowden, Cheshire [189] and in 1850, sold his interest in a Wigan coal mine after a mining disaster.[190] He was later associated with steel, cotton, heavy engineering and shipping.

The Moseley Arms lost its coaching connections before the railways totally replaced the stagecoach, and by 1841 the Royal and the Talbot had most of Manchester's remaining stage-coach business.[191] In that year, the hotel was in the ownership of Mary and James and remained an important venue for auctions, dinners and public meetings.[192] But unsavoury characters could turn up. In 1841, a Mr Nathan, was robbed of £75 at the hotel by George Mottershead and Thomas Millward. James Lyons gave evidence against them.[193] James was employed at the hotel for 35 years until his death in 1869 when he was described as "the faithful servant of the late James Richardson." [196] The last mention of Cumberland John's widow, Mary, is in an advert of 1844 for a sale "by W.H. Fletcher at the house of Mrs Richardson, the Moseley Arms, Piccadilly." [197]

For Manchester's working people, the 1840s were known as the "hungry forties" because of high food prices and low wages, and there was much unrest. The Moseley Arms was patronised by the Chartists, the successors of those who had organised the Peterloo meeting and who continued to press for further Parliamentary reform. In 1839, the liberal reformer, Sir George Murray gave a speech at the hotel attacking slavery which had been abolished in the British Empire; presumably he was referring to the Americans.[198] The Chartists' fiery leader, Feargus O'Connor, was a guest in March 1842,[199] and the next year Charles Dickens turned up.[200] In 1845, a Chartists' Convention at the Carpenters' Hall was followed by a supper at the hotel where O'Connor toasted the "Plug Street Drawers of 1842" and called upon Richard Pilling from Ashton-under-Lyne, "the father of the movement, to speak to his children." [201] The plug drawers sabotaged factory steam boilers by removing their safety plugs. In 1848, the police arrested the radical lawyer, Ernest Jones, in his bedroom at the hotel, on a charge of sedition for a speech he had made in London, probably at the great Chartist rally on the Good Friday of that year.[203] Though of middle class background, being born in Berlin in 1819 where his father was a diplomat, Jones was a champion of the working class. After his conviction, he spent two years in solitary confinement, but emerged to continue the fight. He died in 1869 and was buried at

Ardwick cemetery where a monument was raised to his memory.

A flavour of the Chartists' disrespect for the establishment can be sensed in a scurrilous advert in their newspaper, *The Charter*, on February 3rd 1839.

> *Just arrived, a Huge Rat, the property of the Master Bookbinders Association of London. It is a very intelligent animal, and answers to the name of V.R. It is to be seen at the Mosley Arms Hotel.*

The book-binders were the men who had quarrelled with Bent and Robinson at their book shop in 1825 and it seems their London brethren were equally militant, because V.R. can only mean *Victoria Regina*. The stunt seems simply to abuse the Queen and raises the question of James's politics. Exhibiting a rat in a hotel was in doubtful taste, that open sympathy with republican sentiments might have been bad for the Moseley's business. Like most Mancunians, James supported the Anti-Corn Law League and contributed to one of its demonstrations.[204]

In January 1845, a serious fire in the neighbouring buildings damaged the Moseley Arms. The *Manchester Times* described it in some detail, and mentioned William Rose's part in bringing it under control. "The Mosley Arms Hotel belongs to the executors of the late John Titley Esq.," it reported "…. and is insured for £4,000…..Mr Richardson, the tenant, is insured in the London Corporation office for £3,000…The entire losses are estimated at "£25,000 to £30,000." [205]

Meanwhile, James Chambers flourished and in March 1847, he opened an office in Cross Street.[206] But on October 15th, he died suddenly, aged 58.[207] The *Dumfries and Galloway Standard*, of October 27th reported.

> *ALARMINGLY SUDDEN DEATH – It is our painful duty to record the very sudden death of James Chambers Esq., estate agent and valuer, Pool Street, Manchester. On Friday week, the 15th inst. Mr Chambers had occasion to visit Congleton, Cheshire, and having finished his business, he left Congleton in apparently good health, by the coach which runs between*

that place and Holmes Chapel Station. Having arrived at Chapel station before the train, Mr Chambers requested leave to remain in the coach until it came up, which was permitted; on the arrival of the train the driver opened the coach door to let Mr Chambers out, and to his astonishment found a corpse. We understand the jury have returned a verdict of "death from apoplexy" Mr Chambers was a native of St Mungo, Dumfriesshire. We are sure the sudden and premature death will be lamented by all that knew him

Although James's will had not been formally drawn up, the probate court allowed it to be proved. It involved the executors in much trouble, particularly in establishing title to the various properties and resolving a squabble between the trustees. This kept the lawyers busy at the High Court for over five years, the case being known as Gratrix v Chambers.[208] A small matter involved a certain George Reece, a painter whom Chambers had used for several jobs. After James's death, Reece put in a bill for £200, but without supporting documents. The executors employed an accountant to go through the books and he concluded that Reece owed the estate £10. They sued him successfully in the Borough Court, being represented by J. Cobbett, son of the famous William. [209] Hall and Gratrix also held a sale of some of James's goods, a list of which reveals he had lived well. The newspaper advert listed the items:-

SUBSTANTIAL HOUSEHOLD FURNITURE: Fine toned cottage pianoforte, in rosewood: 300 ounces of richly chased and plain silver plate: a collection of about thirty paintings by old masters: several fine engravings, framed and glazed: capital double-barrelled gun and single ditto: large iron safe: two mahogany glazed book cases and the whole of the office fixtures: excellent four-wheeled Phaeton, by Fogo and Glorge: powerful bay horse 6 years old: capital Drag, nearly new: useful gig: pony Phaeton, nearly new, and very handsome grey pony: set of single and double harness, large new iron weather vane and other effects.[210]

I guess the reference to the 30 paintings as "old masters" was a bit far-fetched, but a note on the will states these items were sold for £7,000; about £400,000 in 2012 money. When the parts of the real estate with uncertain titles were finally resolved by the High Court in 1855, they comprised:

1. Six shops and houses in Oxford Street.
2. Six houses facing Fairfield Street.
3. The freehold of the Stretford Road Inn, Hulme.
4. A building plot in Hulme.
5. 18 chief rents in Hulme worth £254 13s 2 ½ per annum.
6. Seven chief rents in Stanley Grove.
7. Two semi-detached freehold properties in Oxford Road.
8. Ditto.
9. A building plot between Oxford Road and York Place.[212]

James's connections reveal something about the networking that went on in 19th century Manchester. He probably did business with Gratrix regarding building supplies, and John Hall probably knew Gratrix through the metals trade. James shared his interest in Scottish affairs with Barbour and through the Richardsons, he had contacts with the hotel trade: James at the Moseley Hotel: with London publishing through Robert Bent, and with the London wine trade and India via William Barnfield.

But what sort of man was he? It is not easy to know the character of a man who has left no record of his words. He may have been a slum landlord like Gratrix, but his marriage to a woman 26 years his senior is more intriguing. His motive could be better judged if we knew the wealth of each at the time of their marriage. Grace may have had the capital James needed. She was perhaps a good-looking woman; her grand-daughter, Elizabeth certainly was.[213] She may have lied about her age at the 1841 census out of vanity, but it is unlikely that she deceived James on the point. If James were mercenary, then he met fully his side of the bargain, foregoing children and devoting himself to the welfare of his wife's family. That was honourable. But it may have been a love match. Either way, he was a worthy man, and it seems pretty certain that he gave John's children a better start in life that John himself could, or would, have done.

AN AUTUMN MARRIAGE

Gentleman John's remarriage – The Hardy family – All Saints Tavern – Southport – John Hall's success - the lawsuit – Moseley Arms at mid-century – James's death – Betsey Barnfield's return – Changing Times.

Gentleman John almost certainly failed as a solicitor and after five years he fell back on the only other business of which he had any knowledge; inn-keeping. In 1846, as part of this strategy, he married another Elizabeth, the 35 year-old daughter of Hannah Hardy, a widow of Cecil Street, Greenheys.[214] He was 48 and living on Devonshire Street under his old description of "gentleman." [215] For a slightly hard-up man past his prime, a pub and a good woman was not a bad prospect; and perhaps for a spinster nearing forty, a mature gentleman of the road was a fair catch.[216]

Elizabeth brought no dowry. Her father, Matthew, a worthy and honest accountant, had died in 1836, leaving nothing.[217] When Elizabeth was young the family lived in Bedford Street, Chorlton, and Matthew was a partner with James Dale in a Scotch wholesale business at Bridgewater Place.[218] But in 1820, they dissolved their partnership and Matthew went into manufacturing but failed two years later.[220] He then worked as a salaried accountant and joined the committee of the Lancashire Commercial Clerks Society, a body founded in 1802 to aid distressed clerical workers from subscriptions.[221] In 1828, he became its Secretary.[222] In 1835, the Hardys were living at 3, Withy Grove where, on the eve of the Society's annual dinner, their seven year old son, died.[223] In the following July, Matthew made his will and died two days later, aged 56, his passing being "much regretted" for he had carried out his professional duties "with fidelity and attention." [224] His post was advertised immediately and the job description listed the requirements; honesty, competence, account-ancy skills, good references and an upright character. The salary was £60 per annum.[225]

The Society supported Hannah in her distress and she opened a boarding house in Park Street, off Burlington Street, now part of the University campus.[227] Later she moved to Cecil Street, Greenheys, a pleasant thoroughfare lined with fine terraced houses where Frederick Engels, Karl Marx's co-author of the *Communist Manifesto,* lived in the 1860s.[228] A newspaper notice of December 1845 refers to the "residence of Mrs Hardy of Greenheys" where her sister, Jane, died; "wife of George Bolton, stock and share broker, of Liverpool." [229] In short, despite some hard luck, the Hardys were solidly middle class.

The All Saints Tavern, York Street, in the 1960s

John and Elizabeth's wedding took place, by licence, at the Collegiate Church on November 26th 1846, and James Chambers and a certain Samuel Simpson were witnesses. Given John's links to the legal profession and the Hardy family, the likely Simpson was a solicitor with offices at 33, Back King Street who had married a Sarah Hardy of Manchester in 1839.[230] John and Elizabeth then took over the All Saints Tavern, 93, York Street, Chorlton-on-Medlock, a street where 20 years later the future Prime Minister, David Lloyd-George, was born. It no longer exists but it ran parallel to Oxford Road, one block to the east. The district around All Saints was then losing its middle class aspect and industrial buildings and workers' housing were creeping into the green spaces.

In August 1847, Elizabeth gave birth to a son, Charles Henry, but John's joy was jolted on Good Friday 1848, when Mary, his daughter, died.[231] The note on the paper in the family Bible referred to her as Mary Richardson, even though she had become Mary Roberts. I cannot find an official record of her death and the inscription on the Hardcastle vault at St John's, Deansgate, where she was buried, simply refers to "Mary, daughter of John and Elizabeth Richardson." [232] Her husband, Edward, may have died or deserted her. In that year, John's wife had a daughter, Mary Jane, known as Polly; but little Charles Henry died on Oct 10th.

And now we come to another jarring note. A story was passed down to later generations to the effect that John's grown-up children did not like the new Mrs Richardson, whereupon they migrated to Australia. The emigrant must have been John Hardcastle Richardson because Mary was buried at Manchester and Elizabeth remained in England. Moreover, his death in March 1861, noted in the family Bible, does not occur in the official British records. However, despite difficulties with his daughters and the responsibilities of a pub, wife and young family, John still managed to have fun. In June 1849, a sporting newspaper revealed that he was still in the flash set. The June 24th issue of *The Era*, ran the story:

TROTTING AT MANCHESTER: *On Tuesday last, a hastily made match came off on the Cheadle and Rusholme road between Wm. Longden's grey mare, Yorkshire Lass, and Mr Clark's chestnut mare, jocularly termed the cart-mare, to trot 5 miles for 10 sovs a side. The cart mare was in harness and the Yorkshire Lass in saddle; and such was the confidence in the spicy sportsmen assembled, that 2 and 3 to 1 were laid on the cart mare. The odds may be partly accounted for by the grey mare being fresh from grass, and having been*

kicked the day before. The well known Mr John Richardson,
the celebrated livery stable keeper of Salford, [no relation]
mounted the bonny grey and did the knowing, as none but
those who understand horse-flesh can do. The chestnut found
a clever pilot in Mr John Richardson of the All Saints Tavern,
Manchester, and ex-premier of the Peverill of the Peak, with
her owner as his mate. An excellent start being effected, the
grey took the lead for the first mile ... broke from her trot; the
chestnut took advantage of "the chapter of accidents", but
the grey recovered, ... led again, kept well to her work, broke
no more and won the match." .... "Time 17 minutes 30 sec-
onds. A merry meeting was afterwards passed at Mr James
Robinson's.... Boar's Head, Withy Grove, Manchester, where
wine, wit and harmony abounded."

The five miles were along the turnpike from Cheadle, by Parrs Wood, Didsbury and Withington, to the turnpike gate at Platt Fields. The average speed was 17 m.p.h. Fast horses and merry company – our John's great joys. A few months later, *The Era* reported a similar stunt in which a Mr John Richardson wagered 25 sovereigns – but which John was it; livery stable owner or publican? [233] I suspect it was our John, since an addiction to gambling would further explain his chronic financial difficulties and his father's unwillingness to allow him to run the hotel.

Two years later, a second son, William Henry, was born and on October 25th 1852, a boy, christened Robert Bradbury Richardson, arrived. In that year John became a freemason (Lodge of Friendship No 52, Manchester) which suggests he was regarded as "respectable" and the mid-century must have brought him some joy.[234] But in 1853, young William Henry died, aged three, and in April the next year, John went bankrupt when he could not pay his suppliers, George MacGowan, wine and spirit merchant, and Thomas Bake, brewer of Chorlton. In July, he passed the liquor licence to J. Wyborough.

Almost certainly he had lived beyond his means and borrowed on a scale that the pub's income could not meet. Moreover, his advancing age and the deaths of two children must have had some demoralising effect. In 1854, he was 56, which was bordering on old age in those days, and after the deaths of two infants he and Elizabeth must have worried over the fate of young Polly and Robert in unhealthy Manchester. Their only option now was to fall back on the boarding house business, of which Elizabeth had some experience. They moved to North Moels, an old fishing village on the Lancashire coast, then becoming the resort of Southport. It was not far from Chorley and John had probably visited the place in his youth. In the 1850s, hotels, parks and places of amusement were springing up behind the shore and the family moved to a villa at 20, New Bath Street, standing between Lord Street and the beach. Most of these houses remain small hotels, but numbers 18 to 22 have been replaced by the Conservative Club. The American author, Nathaniel Hawthorne, visited Southport at this time and described the scene; organ-grinders, Punch and Judy shows, bathing machines, donkeys and all trappings of the English sea-side, with sneering Yankee condescension; gently mocking both visitors and inhabitants.

Thus at the 1861 census, John was not a "gentleman" but a "lodging house keeper." His demotion hid the fact that Elizabeth was now the breadwinner. However, they kept up appearances and in February 1858, "Mr and Mrs John Richardson" of Southport, attended a Grand Masonic Ball at the Liverpool Town Hall, presided over by the Earl of Sandwich. At the census of 1861, they had two servants and two guests, as well as two nurses who may have been attending a sick member of the family. Their neighbours included a retired cotton manufacturer from Dukinfield and a curate. These genteel surroundings nourished the haughty respectability that later afflicted Polly.

Young Robert's Southport childhood was certainly comfortable, but he complained that his aged father neglected him. This is not surprising since old men do not cope with boisterous boys. Robert's photograph, taken when he was thirteen, shows a smart lad in a light three-piece suit with a watch and chain upon his waistcoat. He was good at school and my father believed he intended to become a Merchant Navy officer. There were several training ships moored in the Mersey and around the North Wales coast, notably the *Conway, Indefatigable, Clarence* and *Akbar*. I have been unable to trace him in any of them, but the idea is credible for North Moels was a small port and Robert would have seen a constant stream of tall ships passing to and from the Mersey.

Meanwhile at the clock and jewellery shop in King Street, John Hall's talents and industry were raising his family from comfort to riches.[235] He and Elizabeth had five daughters, one of whom died in infancy, and a son. Their first surviving daughter, born in 1843, was Elizabeth, who was followed by Emily (1846) and then another girl who was christened Frances Chambers Hall, revealing Elizabeth's affection for her recently deceased step-grandfather.[236] [237] The next daughter, Jessie Margaret (1850) bore the name of James Chambers' niece, Jessie, and finally there was John Henry (1852). The Halls also gave a home to their orphaned niece, Ellen Roberts, who, at the age of 16, was their cook.[238] John Hall always described himself as a silversmith but became a great industrialist. In 1860, he was a director of the Norton Iron Company of Stockton-on-Tees and a partner in Messrs Hall, Poole & Co., cotton spinners, of Adelphi Mills, Salford.[239] In that year he founded the Lancashire Steel Company which obtained the patents on Bessemer's process with the aim of producing 200 tons of steel a week at a 10-acre site in Gorton. The works was built and the furnaces and necessary ancillary machinery installed, but the company seems not to have met its targets and was wound up in 1871.[240] John was also a director of Hopkins, Gilkes & Co., Middlesbrough, and Deputy Chairman of the Beverley Iron and Wagon Works.[241] In 1872, he was Chairman of the Carnforth Building and Gas Co.[242]

After her husband's death, Grace Chambers went to live in Cross Street, but died at the Halls' home in King Street in December 1849, aged 84.[243] Thereupon, John's children refused to pay him the £20 per annum as required by James's will. This must have been with the approval of Hall and Gratrix and led John to sue them. This was not merely a point of honour; he needed the cash. The matter was eventually decided in the High Court of Chancery in 1861 and written up as a law report.[244] The judge, Sir John Stuart found in John's favour and awarded costs against Elizabeth Hall and young Ellen Roberts. It is not quite clear whether John Hardcastle Richardson had paid up, or had died. The ruling provided for £390 for a Mr Thorneley, to whom

John was in debt.[245] The affair reveals the terrible feeling between John and his daughter for her refusal to pay was vindictive. She could have paid him from her house-keeping but it seems she truly despised him. This brings us back to his behaviour after her mother's death, and perhaps earlier. He must have upset her in some very painful way and it is unlikely that her animosity was due simply to a petty dislike of the second Mrs Richardson.

Meanwhile, Uncle James and his sisters continued to run the Moseley Arms. In 1851, their aunt, Alice Barton, born at Chorley and almost certainly his mother's sister, was living with them.[246] But for some reason in the November of that year, the liquor licence passed from James to Mary and Margaret.[247] Was he unwell? The hotel continued to host functions and in February 1852, under a banner heading "Unprecedented attraction – animal magnetism and somnambulism," a hypnotist advertised his services to clients "from 12 to 4 in a private sitting room." [248] In August, there was a picture exhibition.[249] In 1855, an advert for a horse revealed that Cumberland John had retained the old inn's stable block in Market Street. [250] But in 1858 the hotel again passed into the hands of "M. and M. Richardson." [252] Where was James? In 1860, when the building's owners wished to sell the freehold, the rental was £500 per annum, and "Mr Richardson's lease" had two years to run. This suggests that Mary and James had taken out a 30-year lease on Old John's death in 1833.[253] In 1861, the local Volunteers honoured their Captain Porteus with a dinner at the hotel for 50 officers.[254]

At the 1861 census, and again in 1863, James was the head of the household.[255] So if he had been indisposed through illness, he had recovered. At the 1861 census, there were 17 guests, and the three Bent sisters. Betsey was 34, Margaret 32 and Marianne 26. All three were known to Slugg, the Manchester historian, as the "misses Bent" who were active in the Sunday School at St Anne's church.[256] Ten years earlier, Betsey had been a governess to the Rev. John Smart, rector of Kingswear, Devon, where she had charge of eight children.[257]

James died at the hotel of "apoplexy" on April 22nd 1867 in the presence of the faithful James Lyons,[258] and Mary took the business over. Two years later, Marianne Bent died of "atrophy," probably

Piccadilly, Manchester, in 1889: The Moseley Arms Hotel is immediately to the left of the statue.
Reproduced by kind permission of the Francis Frith Collection.

tuberculosis, aged 33.[259] Her death certificate noted her occupation as "daughter of Robert Bent, stationer," which means she had no formal work. At the 1871 census, Mary was there with Betsey and Margaret Bent.[260] Also present was Aunt Betsey Barnfield, now described as an "accountant." It seems that as William Barnfield's fortunes declined, he fought on, delaying the final catastrophe; first in England and then in Calcutta, but ill-fortune caught up and he filed for bankruptcy with the East India Company in 1854.

> *William Barnfield, at present of No 64 Clive street, and late of No 10 Hare street, and previously of No 4, Bankshill street in Calcutta, also of Barrangure, in the district 24 of Pergunnas, Silk Merchant and silk printer, Wine merchant and general dealer, trading under the name of W. Barnfield and Co., filed 19th April.[261]*

He died in December 1857.[262] In the following August, Betsey arrived at Southampton aboard the *Colombo*, having left Calcutta aboard the *Bengal* on July 3rd. [263] The *Bengal* was a modern 3,000 ton, screw-driven steamer in which the orientalist, Sir Richard Burton, had sailed to Arabia five years earlier.[264] Travelling before the Suez Canal was made; she would have left the *Bengal* at Suez and crossed the isthmus to join the *Colombo* at Port Said. She returned to the Moseley Arms to live off her father's trust and keep the accounts. I can find no reference to any Barnfield children. The Moseley Arms must have given a good return in the 1860s, because it sheltered seven of Cumberland John's descendants; James, his three sisters and three nieces. This enraged Gentleman John, who saw them all as spongers off Cumberland John's will trust, though I guess his anger was entirely due to his exclusion from it.

By the end of the 1860s, Manchester was much changed from the day in 1813 when Cumberland John and Margaret had arrived. Not only was the town now "modern," with wide streets and tall, brick buildings, but its life and styles had changed too. Men now wore dark suits with trousers; not breeches and coloured cut-away jackets with gold braid and brass buttons, and women wore hooped skirts, shawls and bustles, not the high-waisted frocks of their grandmothers. Stage coaches had gone and travellers came and went by the railways. The built-up areas to the east and south of the city centre now extended into Clayton and Gorton; and the salmon and trout had vanished from the poisoned and lifeless rivers Irwell and Medlock. But the contrast between the lives of the rich and the workers remained. There had been some improvement in the workers' condition, though Frederick Engels scornfully concluded this was because the shrewder capitalists, having invested in expensive machinery, now needed a better class of worker to operate it. The well-to-do lived in elegant houses staffed by servants in Ardwick, Chorlton, Rusholme and Victoria Park; the workers in over-crowded, insanitary cottages in Hulme, Ancoats, Beswick and Bradford. Comfort and opulence flourished intimately with filth, poverty, disease and wanton violence.

FULL CIRCLE

A reminder – Gorton – Gentleman John's death – Robert let loose – The last Richardsons at the Moseley Arms – The Edlin family – Robert's Royal Navy service – Reddish – John Hall's death – Wealthy cousins – Walter Weblyn – Hulme – Polly's family – Last days of Betsey Bent and Betsey Barnfield – John Richardson IV – Full Circle.

A hundred years after Cumberland John's birth, near a score of his descendants were living, or had recently died. This reminds us of something that those of illustrious lineage often overlook; that our antecedents double with every generation. We have two parents, four grandparents, eight great-grandparents, and so on. If we allow four generations per century, a little arithmetic discloses that five centuries takes us to a million ancestors, amongst whom scoundrels and heroes must be evenly spread. The same is not quite so true with regard to our descendants because of the hazards of reproduction and survival. It reminds us that we, as individuals, are mere focal points in a dynamic inter-flow of genes within the population; a unique coming together, prior to dispersion; an event in time and space. "Out, out, brief candle." We may be precious to our friends and kindred, and perhaps to God, but otherwise irrelevant.

In 1867, when Gentleman John's wife was 56 she began to suffer from cancer.[265] She could not run the boarding house and they needed a more affordable home where they could hang Gentleman John's portrait and survive on his small, private income. Polly, aged 19, was a pupil teacher and 15 year old Robert was intending to become a steam engineer, prior to entering the Merchant Navy. They therefore returned to Manchester and took a house at Napier Street in West

Gorton. That area was then a semi-rural district with fields stretching away south from Hyde Road to Levenshulme and Reddish, whilst to the north Gorton Mills and Beyer Peakcock's locomotive works were obliterating the countryside. The district has now been re-developed, but I recall its 19th century aspect, which persisted into the 1960s. At the junctions of Mount Road, Kirkmanshulme Lane and Hyde Road, there was an amusement park and zoological garden, known as Belle Vue. At its eastern gate was a pub, known as the Lake Entrance, on account of a pool within the boundary. Opposite stood the drill-hall of the Gorton Volunteers and on the north side, two streets, Napier (now Crossley) Street and Cross Lane, led off from each side of the Three Arrows Inn.

Elizabeth was nursed in her last days at Yew Tree Farm, Gorton, where she died on April 29th 1868, attended by Louisa Pickford.[266] For some reason, she was buried at St Paul's, Withington. John was now well advanced into the "natural decay" that ended his days on July 20th of the following year. He was buried at Withington with Elizabeth, near the church door in a grave not now marked by a stone, perhaps because of the refurbishment of the churchyard in the 20th century, or perhaps because Polly and Robert could not afford one.[267] Nonetheless, John's death certificate described him as "Gentleman, Income from Property." But having no real estate, he made no will, and only the income from the Chambers trust and possibly his own annuity, had allowed him to cling to his gentlemanly status. When the payments ceased on his death, there was nothing for his children.

Gentleman John emerges from the records a little more clearly than his father; but whereas the poor Cumbrian lad had succeeded in his business and became a worthy citizen of Manchester; his son seems merely to have posed as a "gentleman." He married young at a time when responsible men did not, and ran through a small fortune by the time he was thirty. His father would not allow him to run the Moseley Arms, nor become a governor of the Royal Manchester Institution. His quarrels with father, stepmother, brother, sisters, and later his own children, point to a volatile and selfish nature, whilst his admiration for Robert Bradbury seems childish. He passed his best years among an energetic Manchester middle class without emulating his father, James Chambers, Sam Gratrix or John Hall and his income probably dwindled over the years. The lawsuit suggests his daughter truly despised him. This evidence is damming and I fear George Borrow's jaundiced portrait of the stage-coachman seems terribly plausible in his case.

In Gorton, Polly found a teaching post and Robert became an apprentice steam engine mechanic, probably at Beyer Peacock's works.[268] After his father's lawsuit, there was no chance of John Hall helping him into a managerial career in one his many businesses.

Moreover, at the age of seventeen, he was freed from any restraint other than that imposed by his slightly older sister and he soon proved to be a chip off the old block; the public house became irresistible for him. Polly bewailed their ill-luck and nursed on her father's grudges and encouraged by his success against the Halls in the High Court, wanted to take legal action over their supposed interest in the Moseley Arms. Several times she cajoled Robert into visiting a solicitor, but he never went further than the pub and eventually gave up on the futile idea. But as Robert's children would later declare, any cash that came his way would have soon vanished.

At the Moseley Arms, Mary and Margaret carried on with the help of the Bent sisters after Uncle James's death. In 1869, Sir Oswald Moseley's agent collected the annual rents at the hotel, where according to custom, the tenants would be given a good dinner after being relieved of their cash.[269] But a court case of 1872 revealed the seamy side of hotel life when Joseph Penkatt, aged 74, and for many years the hotel's night porter, suffered injury at the hands of an unruly guest. One night, a Wolverhampton iron master called Plimley, a regular visitor who held trade shows at the hotel, got drunk and went to bed. Then, stark naked, he left his room and behaved indecently to the head chambermaid. She escaped to old Penkatt who "coaxed" Plimley back to his room; whereupon Plimley rushed out and tossed the old man down the stairs. Joseph sued Plimley, hopefully with the family's help, and won £30 damages.[270]

In October 1872, Mary Richardson died, aged 62,[271] and her sister and Margaret Bent probably died shortly afterwards, for they vanish from the records. Thus by 1873, all Cumberland John's children were gone and Betsey Bent was left to run the hotel with Aunt Barnfield.[272] But coping with naked drunks was most disagreeable for an educated lady and in October 1874, she passed the liquor licence to Jonathon Crowther.[273] This was the point at which Cumberland John's will trust was wound up and the family's tenancy of the Moseley Arms ended. I guess the assets and goodwill were sold to Crowther and the proceeds went to Aunt Barnfield and Cousin Betsey Bent. They probably bought pensions before they retired to Great Cheetham Street, Higher Broughton, on the green and airy regions above the river Irwell.[274]

Crowther ran the hotel until April 1882 when the site was put up for sale.[275] In the early 1890s, the buildings occupied by Cumberland John in 1830 were demolished and a new hotel built in a grand Victorian, red-brick, gothic style. The Mosley Hotel Co. Limited (the middle "e" being finally banished) was formed in 1893 but went broke in 1898.[276]

After Gentleman John's death, Polly and Robert moved from Napier Street to Bowers Street in Gorton where Polly supplemented their income by taking in lodgers.[277] In his little leisure time, young Robert caroused about Hyde Road with a pal, William Hardy Edlin, who was probably a cousin. William's mother, born Lucy Jane Hardy, was probably related to Matthew Hardy.[278] William's father, Ebenezer (1830 - 1878) came from Leicestershire and was a druggist on Piccadilly before qualifying as a surgeon.[279] As a student at the Manchester Medical School, Ebenezer won a prize of five guineas in 1862.[280] He then practised at Middlemoor House, Stockport Road, Levenshulme.[281] William's younger brother, Herbert, also qualified as a doctor from Owens College in 1884 and followed his father in the Levenshulme practice. In 1885, he was appointed surgeon to the Manchester Warehousemen & Clerks' Provident Association's school at Cheadle Hulme,[282] and was for many years the medical officer for the Levenshulme District Council.[283] In keeping with his family's medical tradition, young William became a "surgeon's apprentice" but never qualified and was a surgeon's assistant at his death at Alma Park, Levenshulme, in 1899.[284]

Robert then met a young lady, Elizabeth Hannah Mellor, whose parents, James and Emily, came from Mossley in Ashton under Lyne, where she was born in 1854.[285] In 1871, she lived with her parents and brothers, James and John, and one servant, at Priory House, Reddish, in the shade of Houldsworth's huge mill.[286] The Mellors were cotton spinners and Elizabeth Hannah was a roller-winder.[287] They represented the more fortunate section of the Victorian working class, being decent and literate folk and not the depraved rabble described by Engels.[288] Elizabeth Hannah owned a set of small, leather-bound devotional books; a Bible with a brass clasp, a Book of Common Prayer and a Hymnal.[289] She was devout, very pretty and, according to my father, regarded as the "Belle of Reddish". Her photograph, taken about this time, shows she merited the title.

Robert Bradbury Richardson aged 13 (1865) and
Elizabeth Hannah Mellor at the time of her marriage (1874)

Robert and Elizabeth fell in love, but, according to their daughter, Robert's family did not approve of his marrying a mill girl. This disproval could only have come from Aunt Barnfield and Betsey Bent, since both his parents had died and he remained on good terms with Polly. There may have been some lingering, though strained, connection with the Halls, though I doubt it. Matters came to a head in 1874 when the two Betsey's were selling up the family's interest in the Moseley Arms and if they needed an excuse for not helping Robert, his proposed marriage probably supplied it.

Not to be thwarted of his marriage, but unable to become a Merchant Navy officer cadet due to lack of funds, Robert joined the Royal Navy at Portsmouth in September 1874 for a ten-year engagement.[290] At that time the Navy was making the change from sail to steam power; that is from the wooden ship of the line to the armoured battleship, and Robert's starting rank, "officer in second class" reflected his engineering qualifications. He was soon "acting engine room artificer" in *H.M.S. Asia*. Three weeks after enlisting, he married Elizabeth Hannah at St Mary's, Reddish. She was twenty and he twenty-two and their best man was William Edlin.[291] They then went to Portsmouth where Elizabeth Hannah took lodgings in the parish of St Mary.

The following year Robert transferred to a new frigate, *H.M.S. Sultan* [292] and on August 15th 1875, Elizabeth Hannah gave birth to John William, the first of her ten children. However, she missed her northern home and may have been depressed, so Robert bought his discharge and ended his brief naval career on March 31st 1876. His seniors had found his conduct "exemplary".[293] The only exciting event in his short service was an outbreak of scarlet fever aboard *Sultan* that drove her into quarantine at Plymouth in January 1876.□

They then returned to Reddish where Robert went to work in the engine room of a cotton mill, probably Houldsworth's, where Elizabeth Hannah also worked when not bearing children. Their lives were undoubtedly hard. Mills worked long shifts, often through the night and always began at six each morning. There were no rest breaks; machines were unguarded; holidays few and unpaid; and all lay under the tyranny of the masters. It was a life of drudgery and toil marked by periodic bouts of poverty during the slumps that chronically affected the cotton trade. For Robert, the cosy sitting room with port in the decanter and a maid to fetch it, were gone. He now lived in a back-to-back cottage with one cold water tap and an outside privy. For Cumberland John's male line, clogs to clogs had been just three generations, a literal fulfilment of the old Lancashire saying.

On the other hand, Robert was a skilled artisan and could earn reasonable wages. The engineman of a cotton mill was a petty aristocrat and his domain was off-limits to the operatives. It had the sanctity of a church; high ceilinged with white tiled walls and tall windows that lit up the polished brass and steel of the massive engines whose mahogany panelled fly-wheels could be 20 or more feet in diameter. If Robert were good at his job and prudent in his living, his family might modestly prosper; if not, their lot would be hard.

The working mothers of young children farmed them out to carers. Sometimes these children were kept sedated with alcohol, or opiates, so that some old dame could keep them in order, and occasional accidental deaths revealed the extent of the practice. When John William was three, his mother placed him, with other young children, in the charge of a simpleton youth who taught them to swim in the Reddish canal. John could swim at the age of three and cover a mile when he was six. This activity remained unknown to his parents until one day a man dashed into the mill yard, crying, "Your Jack's in t' cut." Robert dashed out to the towpath to find his little naked child swimming easily through the murky water.

In April 1877, a daughter, Emily Elizabeth was born, and then James (August 1879) and Robert (August 1881). As small children, John and Emily once wandered among the copses of Reddish Vale where they met a group of men holding an illegal bare-knuckle fight. Fearing detection, the men obliged them to stay until the fight was over, but fed them sweets in the meantime.

In the 1870s, Polly married an umbrella maker, James Williams, and they went to live with one servant at 22, Ducie Grove, All Saints.[294] My father believed that James became a manager at the Great Universal Stores in Ardwick, but died, leaving Polly with three young children; Harold (b.1879), Percy (b.1881) and Bessie, (b. after 1881). In her distress, Polly took up the lodging business and moved to a house in semi-rural Rushford Avenue, off Slade Lane in Levenshulme. There she took in commercial travellers and university students, who, in those days, tended to be well-to-do young men. She was near her cousin, Dr Edlin, on Stockport Road and her sons were educated at the Cheadle Hulme School where he held the medi-

Above : John Hall and his wife, Elizabeth (née Richardson)
Below : Jesse Margaret Hall and Walter Weblyn

cal appointment. Unlike Robert, she clung to the pretensions of her youth and her proud bearing was captured in a photograph taken with her grown-up children about 1905.

In these years, the Halls were living on the other side of Stockport. They left King Street in the late 1860s and moved to a splendid new house, Bramhall Lodge, at the junction of Buxton Road (A6) and Woodsmoor Lane, a spot that Gentleman John had driven by regularly in his glory days. The house was, and remains, a massive, three-storied red-brick pile with high gables and tall, mullioned windows. It had a gate house, stable, coach house and a range of servants' cottages. After the Halls, it passed to a Mr Bell, before becoming a convent and then the Stockport Convent High School for Girls. More recently, it has been incorporated into Stockport Grammar School. Though now much altered it was clearly magnificent and Hall probably had it built. The interior has undergone great changes but some rooms have plaster friezes with gothic and naturalistic motifs that anticipate the art nouveau style and were probably made to Hall's design. He had five resident servants and a coachman, whose name, Withnell, hints at some connection with Cumberland John's second wife. [295]

The Halls also acquired another fine house, Min-Y-Garth, Anglesey, a four-storey Italianate villa on the road between Menai Bridge and Beaumaris. It is built into the side of the cliffs overlooking the Strait and was built in 1882 by the Bulkeley estate.[296] He also acquired a steam yacht, a photograph of which was probably taken below the house.[297] But Elizabeth died there in the October of that year and had little enjoyment from it.[298] John remained an active businessman into his last years, being involved in the affairs of the Malta Hydraulic Dock Company in 1884.[299] He died at Bramhall Lodge in 1887, the *Manchester Guardian* noting that had "amassed a large fortune" and supported the Liberal party.[300] The *Manchester Courier* gave the details of his will.[301]

> *Probate has been granted on the will (dated 28th April 1887) with two codicils of Mr John Hall late of Bramhall Lodge, Stockport, the value of whose personal estate has been*

declared at £58,886 19s 3d by the executors, Mr John Sutcliffe, of Lower Lee, Hebden Bridge, Yorkshire, and Mrs Elizabeth Sutcliffe, the testator's daughter. He bequeaths an annuity of £50 for her life to his niece, Miss Ormishe; his furniture and household effects, plate, pictures, horses and carriages and £500 to his daughter Frances Chambers Hall, £500 each to his daughters, Mrs Elizabeth Sutcliffe, Emily, wife of Mr Edgar Poole of Fallowfield, Manchester, and Jessie Margaret wife of William [an error for Walter] Weblyn of 168, Strand, London: and he devises for sale the Bramhall Lodge estate, the proceeds to be held in trust to pay the income for his life, to his son, John Henry Hall, and with the power of appointment to him in favour of his children. From the residue of his estate the testator bequeaths in trust £4000 each for his daughters, the said Mrs Sutcliffe and Miss Francis Chambers Hall and as to the ultimate residue bequeaths one moiety in trust for his said four daughters in equal shares as tenants in common, the income only of the shares to be paid to his said son or his said daughters with powers of appointment in favour of their children.

The estate's value in 2012 terms was between 5 and 24 millions, depending on how the comparisons are made.[302] However regarded it was indeed a fortune. Hall's *Manchester Guardian* obiturist wrote that "In acts of private benevolence he was an exceedingly generous giver…" Well, perhaps he was, but dared not cross his wife in the matter of her father's £60 a year.

In 1876, Sam Gratrix, the other executor of James Chambers' will, lived at West Point in Upper Chorlton Road, Whalley Range.[303] In that year, the notorious criminal, Charlie Peace, attempted to burgle West Point but was confronted by P.C. Cock whom he shot dead. Two innocent men were convicted for the crime on circumstantial evidence and jailed for life. Later, when facing the gallows for other crimes, Peace admitted the murder at West Point.[304] His notoriety long out-lived him; I once heard my Aunt Emily refer to a naughty boy as a "real Charlie Peace."

Of course, Robert and Polly had no friendly dealings with the Halls; their half-sister was some 30 years their senior and her quarrel with their father had begun before they were born. I do not know what became of Ellen Roberts, but the Hall cousins went on to enjoy privileged lives. By the age of 27, young John Henry Hall was a country gentleman at Porthamel Hall, an ancient seat of the Bulkeley family at Llanidan, Anglesey, overlooking the Menai Strait and graced with landscaped gardens.[305] In 1878, his appearance at a ploughing match was noted by the gossip columnist of the *North Wales Chronicle*.[306] Two years later, his wife, "Mrs Harry Hall," sought a housemaid; "Church woman preferred" read the advert, suggesting a "chapel" woman need not apply.[307]

Frances Hall did not marry and lived for many years in Fallowfield near to her sister, Emily, who married Edgar Poole, probably the son of her father's partner in the Adelphi Mills. Elizabeth Hall married John Sutcliffe, a solicitor of Hebden Bridge, Yorkshire, and lived at Low Lee, a house, its own grounds in the valley below Heptonstall village.

The Halls' third daughter, Jessie Margaret, married a most flamboyant fellow about 1870 and went on to a life of pleasure that is worth recounting, if only to make the contrast with the lives of the other folks in this tale. He was Walter Weblyn, a rich London socialite, who was the owner and editor of the *Illustrated Sporting and Dramatic News,* the bible for metropolitan hedonists. [308] He was also a professional baritone, with the stage name Walter Clifford, and had homes in London's Strand and at Rosslyn House, Surrey.[309] The newspapers of the 1880s and 1890s reported his successes as a racehorse owner and his many attendances at dinners patronised by show business *glitterati*.

The Weblyns were frequent guests of Jessie's parents. At the census of 1881, they were at Bramhall Lodge with their children, Kate (b. 1872), Theodora (b. 1876) and Gladys (b.1879) and over the next few years, they divided their ample leisure between London and the Halls' other home in Anglesey, where they often starred in the local social life. At Beaumaris Town Hall in August 1882, there was a "fashionable concert" in aid of the Pentraeth Church, presided over by Lady

Bulkeley, where "Mrs Walter Weblyn ... played the pianoforte." [310] At a similar concert the next year, Walter, assisted by "ladies, including Mrs Weblyn," sang "A Vision of Love" and "The Wishing Cup," and was encored. Then they both sang "Sous les Etoiles" and ended the show with the National Anthem. [311]

In March 1884, the *London Standard* reported a concert promoted by Mr Ambrose Austin at the Royal Albert Hall that featured "the first singers of the day ... Mr Santley and Mr Clifford" who were accompanied by the composer, Sir Julius Benedict. [312] The next week, at the *Temple of Varieties*, Hammersmith, a Scottish Musical Medley, entitled "The Gathering of the Clans," listed Walter in the cast, and in May he and Jessie appeared in a "Shakespearean Tableau" at a Piccadilly theatre. [313]

After these exertions they went up to North Wales and performed the duet "Vieni meco" at Bangor in aid of the training ship *Clio*. [314] The *North Wales Chronicle* reported "The lady's voice, though very sweet, was not strong enough to be heard in all parts of the hall." [315] But Walter was in the top flight of baritones; a stage journalist commenting in 1884 that he was "second only to Santley" and was about to visit America. [316] In early 1885, a charity concert for the Brompton Hospital included the popular operetta "Cox and Box" with Walter in the leading role and Jessie starring in the concert that followed. [317]

But despite all this jollity, the marriage was in peril and later in 1885 the Weblyns divorced after Walter went off with his mistress. During the court proceedings, John Hall claimed Walter owed him £7,800; which was denied. Not surprisingly, Hall regarded Weblyn as a rogue and recorded his claim in the Deed of Separation. [318] Walter was not short of cash and two years later bought Sir John Millais's newly finished picture "Portia" for 2,000 guineas. [319] He made high quality prints from it and issued them with the Christmas number of the *Illustrated Sporting and Dramatic News*. [320] In May 1888, he sat on the committee of the *Drury Lane Theatre*, [321] and in the September, organised an appeal for a groom who had lost a leg whilst rescuing horses from a stable fire in the Strand. [322] Then in October, encouraged by the phenomenal success of *Portia*, he bought the copyright of *Punchinella*, "one of Sir John Millais's most recent works." [324]

After the divorce, Walter and Jessie faded from the newspapers, apart from some references to the proposed merger of the *News* with a ladies' magazine, but he continued to spend lavishly. In May 1889, his horse, *Grouse*, won the Dorney Plate at Windsor and in January 1890, he attended a grand dinner at York.[325] He still owned the *Illustrated Sporting and Dramatic News*" in 1892, when living at Castle House, Hampton-upon-Thames.[326]

In May 1895, Walter was interviewed for a gossipy piece in *The Sketch* magazine. The report carried his portrait which revealed a round face with eyes too close together for an honest man. He sported a walrus moustache and a coat with a thick fur collar. In response to sycophantic questions, he boasted, bragged and name-dropped, relishing his wealth, contacts and the genius of his staff; or rather his genius in employing them. Of his literary editor, Mr C. Kinloch Cooke, "… a capital man for the post, since in addition to his journalistic and editorial experience, he has a large knowledge of sport. He took double honours at Cambridge and would have got his 'blue' as a cricketer but for a football accident. He is quite an authority on yachting, for he was many years private secretary to Lord Dunraven." His artist, John Sturges, was a pupil of Herring's and "the ablest drawer of horses alive." He added, "I am fond of horses and ride and drive a good deal…" The interviewer commented on the photographs of his beautiful house with its superbly furnished rooms that adorned his office. "Yes, that's mine," Walter purred. "I take great interest in it, and love to live with beautiful things round me."

Jessie lived well off her share of the marital assets and entertained guests in the summer season aboard her Thames houseboat, *Reverie*.[327] Their daughter, Katherine, married a lawyer, Mr F.A. Kent, in December 1892,[328] the year in which Walter became a director of the *Brussels Palace of Varieties*.[329] In June 1897, he paid 1,400 guineas for the race-horse *Cristabelle*,[330] and in 1898 was mentioned, probably as a victim, in connection with a fraud case. [331] His daughter, Theodora, married Rupert Tattersall of the famous blood-stock business and Gladys married Kate's brother-in-law, Mr C. W. Kent, who rowed in the winning Oxford boat crew in 1891.[332] The wedding notice appeared in the *Manchester Courier,* suggesting the Weblyns retained their northern connections, probably Jessie's sisters, Emily and Frances, at Fallowfield.[333]

The Weblyns' world was that of the *The Forsyte Saga*; sumptuous, glittering and a long way from the spinning floors of Reddish, which for some reason, Robert and Elizabeth left in 1881, after the birth of their son, Robert. Quitting their home on the edge of the countryside, they moved to 113, Manchester Street, Hulme, a Manchester slum filled with cotton mills and poor housing.[334] They probably went for better pay, but surely suffered from a worse environment. The dirty townscape of those days persisted until the 1950s and merits some description. Around the city centre was a two mile warren of narrow, cobbled streets lit by gas lamps and lined by cramped, terraced cottages. Each row, perhaps a hundred yards long, ended in a pub, or a mean corner shop. These tiny habitations often housed families of a dozen or more, including aged relatives, and diseases were rife. Factories, foundries and chemical works were jumbled among them, pouring out smoke, fumes and foul smells. Churches and schools were fitted into odd spaces and all was covered in black dust. The pictures of L. S. Lowry give some idea of the scenes but tell a great lie with respect to colour; there were no whites, blues or reds; everything was black or brown and far more people thronged the streets than ever he shows. Indeed, I can remember Jackson Street, Hulme, on a hot day in the mid 1950s with literally hundreds of children at play on the cobbles and the taint of unwashed humanity hanging on the air.

After a while, Robert went to Murray's mill in Ancoats and the family moved to 91, Bradford Road, Ancoats, which was perhaps some improvement over Hulme.[335] He finally settled with Saxons, the steam engine makers in Openshaw, and in 1891 he and his family were at 71, Rowsley Street, Beswick.[337] In these years, they had six more children; Frank (1884), Harry (1885), Mary Jane, known as Polly (1887), Tom (1889), Alice (1891) and Ted (1893). Elizabeth Hannah endured her hard life with the stoic courage shown by millions of women in those days. Robert worked diligently enough but remained a feckless drinker and, apparently, something of a womaniser. My father knew him as an "ale can," but being a great prude, never mentioned the women. Alice Morrow, his grand-daughter, told me that she had heard "whispers." [338] It seems that Elizabeth Hannah managed to curb his worst excesses and generally extracted the housekeeping before he escaped to the pub. She remained a devout Anglican, whilst he scorned the Church of England, which, he said, was the greatest landowner in the country that hypocritically begged the pennies of the poor. He despised all convention and even refused to insure for a decent Victorian funeral. "Throw me in the gutter when I'm dead," he declared angrily. "The Corporation will shift me when I begin to stink." Forty years after his death, I showed Polly, his daughter, his photograph taken about the year 1900. At once she quoted her mother's endearing remark, "Our Old Softy," but would not say more about him and I soon realised she resented my enquiries. I then visited Robert's aged sister-in-law, Mrs James Mellor, at her daughter's home on Bradford Road, Ancoats.

> "It's Dick's lad," the daughter explained loudly into the old lady's ear. "He wants to know about Bobby."
> "Bobby!" she cried with a start. "He was the biggest liar in England!" and she turned away in disgust.

Howsoever Robert's children suffered by his boozing, they benefited from the newly-introduced compulsory state education and did not sink into the depravity that raged around them. His boys did not join the "scuttlers," those infamous gangs of working lads who fought murderous battles with each other and the police all over Manchester in the later years of the 19th century. [339] This was due to their mother who ensured they were reared in the Church and put to such trades as cotton spinning and engineering. The three daughters, Emily, Polly and Alice, grew into bonny girls who were married in the Edwardian days. My aunts remembered their grandmother Richardson as a "dainty little thing" who always went outdoors in bonnet, cape and gloves. She remained the strict Christian matriarch and, said Alice Morrow, "ruled them all with a road of iron."

For Aunt Barnfield and cousin Betsey, Robert had only contempt. In 1881, they lived with one servant at 235, Great Cheetham Street,

Higher Broughton, a new street of red-brick villas on the heights above the river Irwell where Betsey Bent was the head of the household.[340] My father thought the younger Betsey, to whom he always referred as "Miss Bent," was the "lady companion" to his great grandmother; but since she had died in 1868, Betsey must have been the companion to her aunt. Aunt Barnfield died in January 1892, "widow of William Barnfield of Calcutta," aged 88 years.[341] She did not leave a will.

Probably about this time, Betsey Bent passed Richard Hough's Bible and Hurd's *Religions of the World* to Robert. As may be imagined, he received them with outright contempt and made a vulgar suggestion as to what the pious lady might do with the sacred volumes.[342] But Elizabeth Hannah received them with due reverence and inserted the births of all her children, leaving spaces for their marriage details. She made no reference to Gentleman John and the entry previous to hers concerned the marriage of Cumberland John's daughter, Ann, to Jean Baptiste de Fiennes in 1837. Probably at this time Betsey also passed over Cumberland John's portrait to be placed beside that of Gentleman John on Robert's narrow walls. My aunts remembered the great gilt frames and the plentiful whiskers that adorned the faces of the two patriarchs.

Betsey's father, Robert Bent, book-seller and stationer of Paternoster Row in the city of London, died in December 1859.[343] His son, William, followed him in the book trade and must have accompanied him about the country, holding sales of prints and publications that were advertised in local papers. But William seems not to have continued in his father's business. He kept in contact with his sisters and moved to Manchester after his father's death. In July 1864, at Birmingham, he married Jane Allen of Leamington,[344] and their daughter, Alice Mary, was born the next year at Clifford Street, Chorlton on Medlock, when William was a "book-seller's clerk."[345] Then in July 1870 he died of "phthisis," or pulmonary tuberculosis, at the age of 39.[346] His widow took up millinery and dressmaking but within three years went broke to the tune of £632, a considerable sum.[347] She continued with her trade, presumably for wages, and Alice followed her. In 1911, when Jane was 78 and Alice 45, they lived in a large house at 242, Brunswick Street.[ ] They had two lodgers, one of whom was Betsey Bent, now aged 84 and "of independent means." She lasted another five years and died on 24th September 1916. Her death certificate did not describe her as a retired governess, but as "a spinster and daughter of Robert Bent, a newspaper editor (deceased)." This was probably Alice's understanding of *Bent's Literary Advertiser*.

On Betsey's death, Cumberland John's estate was finally exhausted. Although she was remembered in the family as the one who had done well out of the Moseley Arms, I suspect her life had not been easy. Her father had worked hard and striven to see his girls well educated and, no doubt, well married. But after losing his wife, he was obliged to rely on the family until they could earn their livings. The life of a governess in Victorian England was genteel drudgery for a cook's pay. They were regarded as too refined to dine with the servants but not good enough to dine with the family; except on special occasions, and they usually ate alone in their attic bedrooms. Most masters did not fall in love with them, like Jane Eyre's Mr Rochester, though often they seduced and discarded them. Moreover, after Betsey returned to the Moseley Arms Hotel in her late forties, she seems to have pulled her weight. I trust she had earned a comfortable retirement.

In the early 1880s, young John William attended St Philip's Church of England School, Beswick, from where in his eleventh year (1886) he went in the afternoons to work at the mill, probably Keymer's in Ancoats. Such children were normally "piecers" who crawled under the clattering machines to "piece," or rejoin, the broken threads and they could be injured in their work. Moreover, a stiff discipline kept them in order. At John's mill, the over-looker carried a stick with which to chastise the children, and once seeing John misbehave in some minor way, gave him a swipe that broke his forefinger.

In August 1888, when he was thirteen, John went to work full time.[348] Thus ended a childhood he remembered as hard and bleak. His father spent his little leisure at the pub and the frequent births of siblings deprived him of his mother's attention. He was left to fend for himself among the swarms of ragged and half-starved children in the back streets of Hulme and Ancoats. He suffered by this neglect but was thoroughly schooled in the Victorian virtues and remained a dutiful son. Moreover, his scant education stood him in good stead; he learned to write a good copperplate script and later read widely. Above all, he learned to be tough.

He worked in the mill for another four years but in 1891, when he was sixteen, his mother's ninth child, Alice, was born and he decided to leave the over-crowded home and go to sea.[349] He was a wiry youth; slim, fair of hair and complexion and more resembling his mother than did his brothers, who inherited their father's short stature and dark, good looks. He stood five feet seven but later grew to six feet.[350] He left home on June 2nd 1892 to walk to Liverpool, much as Cumberland John had left Wigton a century before.[351] His immediate situation was not as grim as his great-grandsire's but there were parallels, for he was penniless and of meagre education, with only his wits and bodily strength to rely on. At Warrington, he came upon Wellington Barracks where the idea of a soldier's life must have suddenly appealed. A regular meal, a warm bed and comrades; what more could a lad want? That day he became 3832 Private John Richardson, 1st Battalion, Kings Regiment (Liverpool) and thus began another story.

LAST WORD

This tale has not been one those Victorian sagas in which the heroes prosper and the villains come to grief; fate seems to have rewarded vice and virtue impartially. Cumberland John triumphed over early misfortunes and after making a good marriage, almost founded a prosperous dynasty. Yet, he lost two children in infancy and his eldest son as a young man. Of his seven surviving children, three did not marry. His male successors, Gentleman John and grandson, Robert, tuned out to be wastrels, but produced seventeen grandchildren between them. Was this reproductive talent written into the Y chromosome that Poor Betty encountered in her misfortune? Of Cumberland John's three married daughters, two married men who went bankrupt and one was childless, though Ann de Fiennes may have had more children after the death of her first born in 1837. At the mid-century, Cumberland John had at least eight surviving descendents. Of them, only Elizabeth Hall, Polly Richardson and William Barnfield Bent had offspring, and his line died out in the next century. Polly's three children never married. John's descendents certainly avoided poverty, but suffered by premature deaths; Alice Bent, aged 34 in 1834, and Elizabeth, Gentleman John's wife at a similar age in 1835. Seven young children in two families were left motherless. Furthermore, the bankruptcies remind us how, in those days, bad-debts and slumps destroyed businesses run by sober and industrious men.

As the century wore on John's descendents spread out along the social spectrum that Benjamin Disraeli characterised as two nations, and snobbery seems to have been the constant imperative behind the process. Gentleman John's posing strikes us as semi-comic; especially as he was not especially well educated and must have spoken broad Lancashire. We wince at Betsey Bent and Aunt Barnfield, the grand-daughter of Poor Betty, sneering at young Robert for marrying a beautiful mill-girl of impeccable manners and character. Moreover, it seems that the success sought by Cumberland John and John Hall was directed at making their sons "gentlemen" – that is fellows who lived in comfort without the need to earn a living. Frederick Engels argued that this evolution, and the sense of injustice that it engendered in the working classes, sapped their patriotism and warped their sense of Englishness. There is some truth in that assertion; but when the call came in 1914, five of Robert's sons enlisted at once, and three paid the patriot's final price.

NOTES and REFERENCES

1   Summerson, Henry, 1993: 'Mediaeval Carlisle', *Cumberland and Westmorland Antiquarian and Archaeological Society,* Extra Series XXV.

2   I concluded this from a search of the parish registers of Caldbeck, Greystoke, Westward, Wigton and Sebergham.

3   The Wigton parish register is the source of information of births deaths and marriages in this chapter.

4   Family Bible.

5   Carrick, T.W., 1992: *History of Wigton*, Bookcase, Carlisle, p 41.

6   Carrick, 1992, *ibid.*

7   Wigton poor records, Cumberland Record Office, Carlisle.

8   Slugg, J. T., 1881: *Reminiscences of Manchester Fifty Years Ago*, J. E. Cornish, Manchester, p.221.

9   Family Bible: Chorley Church Registers. Richard Hough married Alice Ainscow at Chorley 20th Nov. 1764. A Hough family had lived at nearby Croston since Elizabethan days. (Hough family website.)

10 Cobbett, William, 1822–1826, *Rural Rides*, Nelson, London 1920.

11 The date of the death of the first born Betsey on the family gravestone suggests that she was born before her parents' marriage. This was not so, as the parish registers make clear. The mason made a mistake.

12 *Manchester Mercury:* 1st July 1783, Mrs Dean: 6th May 1799 & 9th July 1799, John Crowe: 20th May 1800, H. Darby.

13 Heyes, J., 1994: *A History of Chorley*, Lancashire County Books. All the uncited details of this paragraph are from information in a letter from Mr Heyes and the Chorley Library newspaper cuttings collection.

14 Photograph from the *Chorley Guardian*, 14th Jan. 1937, before the inn's demolition.

15 *Manchester Mercury,* 18th Feb. 1800.

16   Thorne, K.P.C., 1970: 'The Development of Education in Chorley and District from 1800 to 1908.' M. Lit. Thesis, University of Lancaster, p. 16. [Lancashire County Record Office, Preston.]

17   *Manchester Mercury,* 26th August, 1800.

18   For example; *Manchester Mercury:* 10th May 1808, 14th Aug 1810, 18th June 1811, notes auctions at the Royal Oak, and there are others.

19   Below is an advertisement for Mrs Broadbent's charm school for young ladies ridiculed by Mrs Banks in *The Manchester Man*, Abel Heywood, Manchester, 1901.

20   Thorne, 1970: *ibid.*

21   An announcement of John's arrival in Manchester in the *Manchester Mercury*, 11th and 15th June 1813.

22   Marlowe, Joyce, 1966: *The Peterloo Massacre*, Rapp and Whitney, London.

23   Bryant A., 1950: *The Age of Elegance*, Collins, London.

24   Southey, Robert, *Letters from England*, cited by Richard Wright Proctor in *Memorials of Bygone Manchester: With Glimpses of the Environs*, Palmer and Howe, Manchester, 1880.

25   Macaulay, Thomas Babington, 1829: 'Robert Southey,' in *Literary Essays*, George Routledge, London.

26   Southey, Robert, cited in *The Collected Works of Samuel Taylor Coleridge: Lectures 1808–1819 on Literature'*, ed. R.A. Foulkes, Routledge, Kegan Paul, 1987, Princeton University Press.

27   *Manchester Collectiana*, Vol. 68, p 161, Lancashire Record Office Preston: *Manchester Mercury*, 11th June 1813*: Pigot's Directory of Manchester and Salford* (1813).

28   *Manchester Mercury,* 1st March 1808, 25th Sept. 1810: 3rd June 1810.

29   See *Views of the Ancient Buildings of Manchester* by John Ralston, Printwise Books, Hugh Broadbent, Oldham 1989; and J. T. Swindells (1906-1908): *Manchester Streets and Manchester Men*, (2) 34, J. E. Cornish, Manchester. *Baine's Directory of Manchester* (1825) notes the Mosley Arms at 63, Market Street and David Holt at 63a.

30   Swindells: *ibid.* (2) 98–99.
31   *The Manchester Man,* Mrs G. Linnaeus Banks, Abel Heywood, Manchester, 1901.
32   Family Bible: Chorley church gravestone.
33   Chorley church gravestone.
34   Lister, A., (undated): *I Know My Own Heart: The Diaries of Anne Lister 1791–1840*: Ed. Helen Whitbread, New York University Press, 1992.
35   Mrs L. Banks, *The Manchester Man,* Abel Heywood, Manchester, 1901.
36   *Manchester Times,* 8th April 1848.
37   Family Bible: Registers of St John's, Deansgate: John Hardcastle (1769–1804) was a cloth dresser who died of "decay" at the age of 35. The Hardcastles' first child, Ann was born in 1790, so they must have married about 1789. They had three more daughters, Mary (1790–1822) presumably a twin who married John Phillips: Elizabeth (1793–1793); Elizabeth (1800–1834) who married our John.
38   John's will, 1833, Lancashire County Record Office, Preston.
39   *Lancaster Gazette,* 6th Oct. 1821.
40   A royal warrant, now in my possession.
41   Dallas was a distinguished lawyer who had defended Warren Hastings at his impeachment in the 1780s. He became Chief Justice of the Common Pleas until he retired due to ill-health in December 1823. [*Dictionary of National Biography, 1885–1900, Vol. 13*]. He signed John's certificate in June 1824 and died the following Christmas.[*Morning Post* 27 Dec. 1824.]
42   *The Gentleman's Magazine* (1831), Vol. 150, p.187; Swindells: *ibid.* (2) 190–191.
43   *Morning Post,* July 26th 1831.
44   Swindells: *ibid.* (2) 190–191.
45   *Gentleman's Magazine, ibid.*
46   Swindells: *ibid.* (2) 191.
47   *The Gentleman's Magazine, ibid.*
48   McConnel Stott, Andrew, 2009: *The Pantomime Life of Joseph*

Grimaldi, Canongate Books, Edinburgh, p 192 & 256.

49   McConnel Stott: *ibid.*

50   McConnel Stott: *ibd..*

51   'Ryley's Itinerant in Scotland', in *The Kaleidoscope: or Literary and Scientific Mirror*, Vol. 8 (1828), E. Smith, Liverpool, pp. 101–102.

52   Ryley 1828: *ibid.*

53   Jem Belcher, famous heavy weight pugilist.

54   Swindells: *ibid.* (2) 190–191.

55   Swindells: *ibid.* (1) 221.

56   The information in this paragraph is from McConnel Stott, *ibid.*

57   *Manchester Mercury*, Nov. 19th 1811.

58   Procter, 1880: *ibid.* 63.

59   *Manchester Courier,* Nov. 10th 1827.

60   *The Gentleman's Magazine, ibid.*

61   Southey, R., 1808: *ibid.*

62   Ryley, 1828: *ibid.*

63   *Manchester Trades Directory:* 1833. John I's will, 1833, Lancashire County Record Office, Preston.

64   Cobbett, William, 1822–26, *Rural Rides.*

65   *Manchester Courier,* 15th Jan. 1825; John Richardson's will, *ibid.*

66   Marfleet Family website.

67   Banks, Mrs G. L, (1901), *ibid..*, gives a vivid picture of Manchester life in the 1820s.

68   Slugg J.T., *ibid.*, p. 211.

69   Lister, A., (undated): *ibid.*

70   *Manchester Courier,* 30th May 1829.

71   Family Bible & John's will, 1833.

72   Slugg, 1881: *ibid.* Brake, Laurel: *Dictionary of 19th century Journalism in Great Britain, & Ireland*, Marysa Demoor.

73   Brake, Laurel. *ibid.*

74   *Law Advertiser,* 1824.

75   *Manchester Courier,* 2nd April 1824.

76   Slugg 1881: *ibid,* 87.

77   *Manchester Courier*, 15th Jan. 1825.

78   *Manchester Courier,* 26th March 1825.

79   *Manchester Courier,* 16th June 1827.

80   Slugg (1881) confused John and James Richardson and also referred to Thomas Bent as the father of John's nieces.

81   She was a 24 year old governess for the Rev. John Smart at Kingsweir, Devon, at the 1851 census.

82   She was at the Moseley Arms Hotel at the 1851 census, aged 22.

83   St John's Church Register. The 1851 census notes that Marianne and Margaret Jane Bent, then at the Mosley Hotel, were born in Middlesex.

84   British Families in India Society (fibis) website.

85   Asiatic Register: British Families in India Society (fibis) website. Under births at Calcutta, "Mrs Barnfield, a son."

86   *Morning Post,* 17 Feb. 1803.

87   British Families in India Society (fibis) website : Miscellaneous Bonds 1814–1865).

88   *Asiatic Intelligence, Bombay'* 1825 (via internet).

89   *Perry's Bankrupt Gazette* 29th July 1837: *London Gazette,* 18th July 1837.

90   Family Bible and Chorley Church register and tombstone.

91   At the 1841 census, the children's ages are unreliable. Their grandmother claimed to be 60 when she was 75 and told the clerk the girls were teenagers.

92   *Manchester Courier*, March 11th & 25th 1826: Nov 4th 1826: April 21st 1827: Jan 19th 1828: Feb 16th 1828. *Manchester Mercury*, 4th March 1826. *Manchester Courier*, 21st April 1827. The Princess Street practice was in the hands of a John Richardson 50 years later and so may have been a family business.

93   The marriage was by licence with one witness, Nancy Jackson.

94   *Manchester Courier*, 19th Jan. 1828: There are no further references to John Richardson, solicitor. To be found in the on-line National Newspaper Archive until 1841.

95   *Manchester Courier,* 28th June 1828.

96   Alice Morrow, daughter of Robert Richardson (1881–1915).

97   *The Era,* 27th June 1849. John is identified by the reference to the All Saints Tavern.

98   *Wikipedia* cites several primary sources for gentlemen coachmen, including 'Driving Clubs Old and New,' Beaufort, H.C.F.S.: Longmans Green & Co., London 1889.

99   Slugg, 1881, 211 – 218.

100   *Manchester Courier*, 5th May 1829.

101   Swindells, *ibid.,* (2) 99. Slugg, 1881, *ibid.,* 39.

102   Pigot & Smith's map of 1830, in Slugg, 1881, *ibid.*

103   The 1850 OS Map and Frith's photograph of Piccadilly in 1887, in P. Zeigler's *Britain Then and Now*, Weidenfield & Nicholson, London.

104   Notice of auction in the *Manchester Courier,* 25th April 1882.

105   *Manchester Courier,* 27th Feb. 1830.

106   Swindells, *ibid.,* (2) 73.

107   Johann Heinrich Meidinger (1792-1867) cited in 'Visitors to Manchester from 1538 to 1865', D.L. Bradshaw, published by Neil Richardson, Manchester, 1987.

108   De Tocqueville, Alexis, 'Journeys to England and Ireland', 1835.

109   Swindells, (i), 227 and (ii), 97-98.

110   Chorley parish register and tombstone in the churchyard.

111   The will bears a note that the codicil was invoked on May 28th.

112   I have searched the National Newspaper Archive and found only this example.

113   Cruikshank, George & Robert, 1827: *The Gentleman's Magazine*, cited on website, twonerdyhistorygirls.blogspot.co.uk

114   Swindells, *ibid.* (2) 230.

115   *Manchester Courier*, 28th June 1828 (citing the Chesterfield Gazette).

116   Morley, John, 1905: 'Life of Richard Cobden', T. Fisher Unwin, London.

117   *Manchester Courier*, 8th May 1829.

118   *Leicester Journal,* 25th June 1830.

119   Anonymous: *New York Times*, 17th Aug. 1879, via website for *New York Times* archive.

120   Slugg, 1881, 213.

121   *Derby Mercury* 24th March 1830; *Manchester Courier* 20th May 1830.

122   *Chester Courant,* 14th June 1831.

123   *Morning Post,* 12th Dec. 1831; *Chester Courant,* 13th Dec. 1831.

124   Picture is in the Yale Collection of British Art, USA, accessible via the internet.

125   *Northampton Mercury,* 7th Feb. 1835; *Huntingdon, Bedford and Peterborough Gazette*, Oct. 17th 1835

126   *Leicester Chronicle,* Dec. 18th 1830.

127   *Leicester Chronicle,* 15th March 1834.

128   *Leicester Chronicle,* 5th Feb. 1831.

129   *Devon & Wiltshire Gazette*, 17th Feb. 1842 and other newspapers.

130   St John's Church Register and Owen's manuscript respecting Elizabeth's internment in 1835.

131   Slugg, 1881, 215, *ibid.*

132   St John's, Deansgate, Registers.

133   I have been unable to find documentary proof of the marriage but later circumstantial evidence confirms it.

134   1841 census.

135   Information on Robert Lodge (1816-1888) from his gravestone in Aysgarth churchyard and obituary in the *Manchester Courier*, 19th Sept. 1888. The Rookery was demolished in 1922.

136   Bamford, Samuel, 1884: *Passages in the Life of a Radical*, Oxford University Press, 1984, p 360.

137   From the tale of 'Pauline Peronne' in the *Poetic Rosary*, via website, gerald-massey.org.uk

138   *Morning Post,* 30th Dec. 1836: Derby Mercury, 4 Jan. 1837.

139   This portrait perished at the hands of his grand-daughter Polly in 1925.

140   Newspaper stamp duty statistics in the *London Standard*, 6th

Oct. 1835. These sales were about half of those of the *Literary Gazette*.

141   His date of birth is inferred from his daughter's birth certificate; Alice Mary Bent, born 1865.

142   *Morning Chronicle,* 27th March 1834. The 1851 and 1861 censuses record Marianne at the Moseley Arms Hotel, born in Middlesex.

143   *Manchester Courier,* Sept. 6th 1834.

144   *Perry's Bankrupt Gazette*: May 25th 1839.

145   *Dictionary of National Biography*: *Cambridge Bibliography of English*, Vol. 4, (1800-1860), 85, 86.

146   Slugg (1881, 87) confused James with John and incorrectly referred to Thomas Bent as the father of John's nieces.

147   1841 census.

148   *Perry's Bankrupt Gazette*: 9th Jan. 1830: 10th Nov. 1832: 13th July 1837: 23rd June 1838: 16th Feb. 1842: 30th April 1842: 10th June 1843: 27th Dec. 1845.

149   *London Gazette,* 25th July 1854.

150   *Manchester Trades Directory, 1833.*

151   Ellwood, Willis J., *Some Manchester Doctors*, a biographical collection to mark the 150th anniversary of the Manchester Medical Society.

152   *Manchester Weekly,* 21st Aug. 1891.

153   Fitzlyon, April, 1987: *Maria Malibran: Diva of the Romantic Age*, Sovereign Press, London. I have relied mainly on this book for all the details of Maria's life and death.

154   Bushnell, Howard, 1979: *Maria Malibran: A Biography of the Singer*, Pennsylvania State University Press.

155   *London Standard,* 13th Sept. 1836.

156   *The Champion,* 2nd Oct. 1836.

157   *Morning Post,* 15th Oct. 1836.

158   *Manchester Times,* Dec. 12 1836.

159   *The Literary Gazette,* 1837: Vol. 20, 685.

160   *Manchester Courier,* 28th Aug. 1838: "On the second inst., at Brussels, the lady of Mr J.B. De Fiennes, a son. The boy's death

was reported on 8th Sept. 1838.

161   *Manchester Courier,* 20th Dec.1847: *Dumfries and Galloway Standard,* 27th Oct.1847.

162   Grace Chambers' death certificate 1849. I have not seen documentary evidence of a wedding that confirms Grace was formerly surnamed Hardcastle, but all the circumstantial evidence points to it.

163   *Manchester Mercury,* 29th June 1813.

164   *Manchester Times,* 13th May 1840. *Pigot & Slater's Trades Directory of Manchester. Manchester Courier* 18th June 1840.

165   *Manchester Courier,* 25th March 1837.

166   Swindells, (ii) 12.

167   *Manchester Courier,* 14th April 1838, 4th May 1838.

168   *Manchester Times,* 8th July 1843.

169   Marriage certificate.

170   1861 census when she was living with the Halls at King Street.

171   Elizabeth's Marriage certificate and notice in the *Preston Journal,* 11th Dec. 1841.

172   The girls' marriage certificates. Jessie was mentioned as James's niece in his will (proved 1847).

173   *Leicester Chronicle,* 22nd July 1837.

174   *Derby Mercury,* 27th March 1839; *Manchester Courier,* 29th Sept. 1839.

175   *Derby Mercury,* 3rd June 1840. The last four-horse stage coach, "the old Derby mail," left Manchester on Saturday, October 2nd, 1858: *Cheshire Observer,* 9th Oct. 1858.

176   *The Era,* 24th June 1849.

177   Borrow, George, 1857: *The Romany Rye.*

178   Collins, Wilkie, *The Last Stage Coachman,* ebooks@adelaide, 2013.

179   James's will, proved 1847 and the 1861 court judgment referred to below: £670 in 1850 is about £30,000 today: National Archive converter.

180   www.oldchorlton.inc.uk; *Pigot's Commercial Directory* (1818).

181   *Manchester Courier*, 29th Aug. 1849.
182   *Manchester Courier*, 19th Dec. 1835: *Manchester Times*, 26th July 1845.
183   *Manchester Guardian*, obituary, August 23rd 1887; gives the other facts not otherwise referenced in this section.
184   John Hall's marriage certificate, Dec. 2nd 1841: 1851 census.
185   The premises were at No 68 (www.silvercollection.it). At 1841 census, John lodged with Hatfield. Slugg (1881 p. 173) lists a certain John Hall in the congregation of the Cross Street Chapel at this time. He may therefore have been a Unitarian.
186   Loomes, Brian, (1975): *Lancashire Clocks and Clockmakers*, David & Charles, Newton Abbot.
187   *Manchester Courier*, 20th July 1844.
188   *Manchester Courier*, 28th April 1847.
189   County Record Office, Preston: DDX/116/1814.
190   County Record Office, Preston: DDX/116/69.
191   *Pigot and Slater's Directory of Manchester* (1841) C.R.O. Preston.
192   *Pigot & Slater's Directory,* 1841, i*bid.,*
193   *Manchester Times,* 11th Dec. 1841.
194   *Manchester Courier,* 12th Dec. 1869.
195   *Manchester Courier*, August 31st 1844.
196   *North Wales Chronicle*, 10th Sept. 1839.
197   *Manchester Courier*, 12th March 1842.
198   Mentioned in *The Letters of Charles Dickens*, by Chas. Dickens, *et al*, Oxford University Press, 1965, 582-3.
199   *The Northern Star;* 27th Dec. 1845: cited by Malcolm Chase in *Chartism: a New History*, Manchester University Press.
200   Swindells, *ibid.* (2) 99.
201   *Manchester Courier,* 1st Aug. 1846.
202   *Manchester Times,* Jan. 25th 1845.
203   *Manchester Courier*, 25th March 1847; *Manchester Times*, 4th Dec. 1847.
204   *Manchester Courier*, 20th Oct. 1847.
205   The newspaper references to *Gratrix v. Chambers* are too

numerous to list but in 1855, the properties were put up for sale: *Manchester Courier*, 14th April 1855.

206   *Manchester Courier*, 21st Feb. 1849: *Manchester Times*, 20th Feb 1849.

207   *Manchester Courier*, 20th Nov. 1847: The Phaeton, Drag and gigs were horse drawn carriages.

208   *Manchester Courier,* 14th April 1855.

209   A photograph of about 1860 belonging to Mr Stephen Kent; personal communication.

210   Her marriage and death certificates. Matthew Hardy's will: Lancs. Record Office.

211   Marriage Cert.

212   Age from 1841 census.

213   Matthews's will. 1836.

214   Registers of St Luke's, Chorlton on Medlock: a baptism on April 4th. *Pigot's Commercial Directory* (1818) p. 325.

215   *Lancaster Gazette,* 7th Oct. 1820; *Stamford Mercury*, March 1st 1822.

216   *Manchester Courier*, Aug. 11th 1827. Baines, Edward (1836): *History of the County Palatine of Lancaster*, Vol. 2, p. 143. Wheeler, J., (1836): *Manchester: Its Political, Social & Commercial History*, Love & Barton, Manchester, p. 40. The Society's archive is in the Manchester Central Library. Its reserve fund in 1836 was £18,000 and it had disbursed an average of over £900 per annum since its inception.

217   *Manchester Courier,* Sept. 13th 1828.

218   *Manchester Times,* Nov. 6th 1835. The reference to Matthew as an accountant is on Elizabeth's marriage certificate. *Manchester Times,* Nov. 7th 1835.

219   Registers of St Luke's, Chorlton on Medlock. *Manchester Courier,* July 23rd 1836.

220   Minute Book of the Lancashire Commercial Clerks' Society Meeting, 12th August 1836: Greater Manchester County Record Office. The Society's Chairman in 1845 was Robert Barbour, James Chambers' friend: *Manchester Courier,* 9th Aug. 1845.

221   Minute Book of the Lancashire Commercial Clerks' Society Meeting, 21st July 1836: Greater Manchester County Record Office. *Pigot and Slater's Directory of* Manchester (1841) notes Mrs Hannah Hardy at Park Street, Greenheys.

222   Cooper, Glynis (2002): *The Illustrated History of the Manchester Suburbs*, Breedon Books, Derby, p. 112.

223   *Manchester Courier,* 13th, Dec. 1845.

224   *Manchester Courier* 13th March 1839. *Manchester Times,* 18th Nov. 1847 and other legal notices in the Manchester Press.

225   Family Bible: Death cert.

226   This inscription, as recorded by Owen, is also an error, giving the date as 1847. Good Friday fell on April 21st in 1848, not 1847.

227   *The Era,* 25th Nov. 1849.

228   John's Certificate of Freemasonry.

229   Noted on a paper in the Family Bible and on the death certificate.

230   *Perry's Bankrupt Gazette,* 6th May 1854.

231   *Manchester Courier,* 29th July 1854.

232   Aughton, P., (1988): *North Moels and Southport: a History*, Carnegie Press, Preston.

233   Information from (www,oldmserseytimes.co.uk)..

234   My Auntie Alice and her cousin, Mrs Alice Morrow, both commented on their great Aunt Polly's proud bearing.

235   1861 census.

236   1871 census.

237   Frances Chambers Hall lived for some years at Willow Place, Withington, and died in 1925 at a house on Oxford Road, leaving an estate of £3049-15s-7d: Research by Miss T. Szczepanik, a descendant of John Hall's brother, William, personal communication.

238   1861 census: The other cook was Mary Allenby, also born at Cliff, near Selby.

239   *Manchester Guardian,* 23rd Aug. 1887.

240   Wikipedia, citing Lang, E.F: 'The Old Lancashire Steel Company: A forgotten episode in the industrial history of

Manchester', *Proceedings of The Manchester Literary & Philosophical Society,* (1938), pp. 79-93. *Manchester Courier,* 12th Oct. 1867.

241   *Manchester Courier,* 17th Jan. 1865,

242   *London Gazette,* 19th March 1872.

243   Death notice in the *Manchester Courier,* 22nd Dec. 1849. Grace's Death certificate.

244   The details emerge from James Chambers' will and the appeal judgment recorded in *Adjudged in the High Court of Chancery by Vice-Chancellor, Sir John Stuart,* by J. W. Longuville Gifford, Vol. II, 1860–1861, Wildy & Sons, Lincoln's Inn Archway, London, pp. 321–323.

245   For some reason the case was reported as "Gratrix versus Chambers."

246   1851 census.

247   *Manchester Times,* Nov. 19th 185.

248   *Manchester Times,* Feb. 22nd 1852.

249   *Manchester Times,* Aug. 14th 1852.

250   *Manchester Times,* Dec. 18th 1855.

251   *Manchester Trades Directories.*

252   *Manchester Courier,* 17th March 1861.

253   *Manchester Times,* 27th April 1861.

254   *Manchester Trades Directories.*

255   Rev. John Richardson was incumbent in the 1850s. Slugg (1881, p. 87): *ibid.*

256   1851 census: My father's Aunt Polly told me Betsey was a governess.

257   James's death certificate, 1867.

258   Marianne's death cert: died 8th May 1869.

259   The 1871 census noted eleven servants at the Mosley Hotel.

260   *London Gazette,* 25th July 1854.

261   *Allen's India Mail,* 1858, via fibis website.

262   *Hampshire Advertiser,* 21st Aug. 1858. *Calcutta Directory 1858,* via fibis website.

263   Burton, Richard, *Personal Narrative of a Pilgrimage to*

Al-Madhina and Meccah, 1855.

264   Elizabeth's death certificate (April 29th 1868) notes she had been ill for 2 years.

265   Elizabeth's death certificate, *ibid.* Yew Tree Farm was the birthplace of John Higson (1825–1871) author of the *Gorton Historical Recorder* and *The History of Droylsden* (1859): cited by Farrer W. & Brownbill J., Victoria County History: *A History of Lancashire,* Vol., 4, p. 279, (1911).

266   Information from the Rector's plan of the graves.

267   1871 census.

268   *Manchester Courier,* 27th March 1869.

269   *Manchester Evening News*, 24th Aug. 1872.

270   *Manchester Evening News*, 15th Oct. 1872.

271   *Manchester Evening News*, 12th Feb. 1873.

272   *Manchester Courier,* 17th Oct. 1874.

273   1881 census.

274   *Manchester Courier,* 25th April 1882.

275   National Archives, No BT31 / 5731.

276   1871 census.

277   1861 census.

278   1861 census: *Manchester Times* 26th Jan. 1878.

279   *Manchester Courier,* 11th Jan. 1862.

280   *Manchester Times,* 26th Jan.1878: 1871 census.

281   *Manchester Courier*, 4th April 1885.

282   John Rylands University Library website, via ancestry.com

283   1871, 1881, 1891 censuses: *Manchester Evening News*, 1899.

284   1871 census: James Mellor was born 1824 and Emily in 1825.

285   1871 census.

286   Information from her daughter, Polly, about 1970.

287   Engels F., 1892: *The Condition of the Working Class in England*, Granada Publications (1969).

288   Now in my keeping.

289   Robert's naval papers are the source of information for un-cited statements in this and the next paragraph.

290   Marriage certificate.

291   H.M.S. Sultan enjoyed a long life as an engineer training ship and was scrapped in 1945: *British Battleships*, by O. Parkes, cited in *The Hunting of Force Z,* by Richard Hough, Collins, London, 1963.

292   Robert's naval papers.

293   *Edinburgh Evening News*, 18th June 1876. *Sheffield Independent,* 10th Jan. 1876.

294   1881 census.

295   1871 census.

296   Mr John Royle, present owner : personal communication, 2012.

297   Photograph owned by Stephen Kent, John Hall's descendant via the Weblyn – Kent line.

298   *Manchester Courier,* 4th Nov. 1882.

299   *London Gazette*, 22nd July 1884.

300   *Manchester Guardian*, 23rd Aug. 1887.

301   *Manchester Courier*, 3rd Nov. 1887.

302   National Archives money converter.

303   njy98@nickyoung.freeserve.co.uk

304   *Wikipedia.*

305   Censuses of Wales, 1881, 1891, 1901, and research by Miss T. Szczepanik. See above.

306   *North Wales Chronicle,* 12th Jan. 1878.

307   *North Wales Chronicle,* 25th Dec. 1880.

308   Founded in 1874, probably bought by Walter in 1876: *Wikipedia.* Walter Weblyn was born at Peckham, Surrey, in 1846: He was at Bramhall Lodge, aged 39 at the 1881 census: 1911 census states he was born 1854 and at his death he was reported as being born in 1850. A liar about his age?

309   *London Daily News,* 6th Feb. 1889.

310   *North Wales Chronicle,* 26th Aug. 1882.

311   *North Wales Chronicle,* 1st Sept. 1883.

312   *London Standard,* 15th May 1884.

313   *The Era,* 8th March 1884. *London Standard*, 24th May 1884.

314   *Liverpool Mercury*, 26 July 1884.

315   *North Wales Chronicle,* July 26th 1884.

316   *The Otago Witness,* 1884, p. 23.

317   *Morning Post,* 6th Feb. 1885.

318   Dated August 6th 1885, Stephen Kent, personal communication, by email.

319   *Manchester Courier,* 3rd Nov. 1897. *Lloyd's Weekly Newspaper,* 25th Nov. 1887.

320   *The Star,* 22nd Sept. 1887: The picture is now in the New York Metropolitan Museum of Art.

321   *The Era,* 12th May 1888.

322   *Morning Post,* 1st Sept. 1888.

323   *Northampton Mercury,* 13th Oct. 1888.

324   *Sheffield Independent,* 25th May 1889. Walter's horses Ghost and Fanny Burney ran at Brighton (*Manchester Evening News,* 7th Aug. 1892) and at Gatwick (*Liverpool Mercury,* 7th July 1897). *York Herald,* Jan 4th 1890.

325   *Huddersfield Chronicle,* 9th Dec. 1892. *Morning Post,* 27th Feb. 1890.

326   *London Daily News,* 7th Sept. 1893.

327   *London Daily News,* 27th Dec. 1892: Kate was a pioneer of motoring.

328   *Manchester Courier,* 9th Dec. 1892)

329   *Dundee Courier* 29th June 1897.

330   *Morning Post,* 21st Nov. 1893.

331   Mr Stephen Kent (2012), personal communication. *Manchester Courier,* 9th Feb. 1905.

332   Jessie died in 1916 at East Molesley: Walter died at Romford, Essex, in 1928: Genesunited website.

333   1881 census. Alice Morrow told me her father, Robert, was born at Reddish, and he is listed among Stockport's dead of the 1914-18 War,

334   Young John's Labour (school leaving) certificate, 1888. From Auntie Nellie.

335   1891 census.

336   Alice was the daughter of Robert's son, Robert Henry (1881

– 1915).

337   For an account of the scuttlers, see *The Gangs of Manchester*, by Andrew Davies, Milo Books, Preston, 2008.

338   1881 census.

339   *Manchester Courier,* 23rd Jan. 1892.

340   His daughter, Polly, personal communication.

341   On Dec. 6th, *Dictionary of National Biography*.

342   Ancestry.co.uk, index of births, deaths and marriages.

343   Alice Mary's birth certificate 1865.

344   William's death certificate.

345   *Manchester Evening News*, 29th Nov. 1873 * 10th Jan. 1874.

346   1911 census.

347   Death certificate.

348   John's Labour (school leaving) Certificate, 1888. I think he went to Keymer's Mill in Ancoats.

349   Most of the information on John's life is from my father.

350   John's Army discharge papers overlook his growth during his service.

351   John's notebook, *ibid.*

INDEX of PEOPLE

GENERAL INDEX

A 6 road route, 45, 85.
Adelphi Mills, Salford, 73.
Akbar, ship, 72.
Albion Hotel, Birmingham, 31.
Albion Hotel, Manchester, 33, 39.
All Saints Tavern, Manchester, 69–71.
Aldine Chambers, Paternoster Row, 49.
Alma Park, Levenshulme, 81.
Altrincham, 62.
Amphitheatre, 27.
Ancoats, Manchester, 8, 9, 22, 23, 76,
    90, 91, 93.
Angel Inn, Liverpool, 30.
Anglesey, 85, 87.
Anti-Corn Law League, 45, 64.
Ardwick, Manchester, 20, 22, 38, 39,
    48, 61, 64, 76, 83.
Art Gallery, Manchester, 30.
Ashton-under-Lyne, 63, 81.
Asia, HMS, ship, 82.
Astley Estate, Dukinfield, 21.
Australia, 70.

B

Babylon Brow, 22.
Bakewell, Derbys., 45.
Bangor, N. Wales, 88.
Bankshill St., Calcutta, 75.
Barrangure, India, 75
Beaumaris, Anglesey, 85, 87.
Bedford, 45.
Belle Vue, Gorton, 78.
Bengal, ship, 76.
Bent's Literary Advertiser, see *Monthly
    Literary Advertiser.*
Berlin, 63.
Beswick, Manchester, 9, 76, 90 93.
Beverley Iron & Wagon Works, 73.
Beyer Peacock & Co., 79.

Bible, (Richardson Family), 9, 16, 17,
    33, 57, 70, 92.
Birmingham, 30, 31, 92.
Bishopdale, 48.
Black Bull, Preston, 30.
Blackburn, 9, 18, 31.
Blanketeers, 25.
Boar's Head Inn, Manchester, 71.
Bolton, 15, 31.
Bookbinders, 33, 34, 64.
Bow Street, London, 28.
Bowden, Altrincham, 62.
Bradford, Manchester, 8, 76.
Bramhall Lodge, Stockport, 85–87.
Bridgewater Arms Inn, Manchester,
    23, 33.
Brighton, races, ref 324.
Brompton Hospital, 88.
Brussels, 56.
Brussels Palace of Varieties, 89.
Bulkeley Estate, Anglesey, 85.
Bull's Head Inn, Macclesfield, 31.
Bull's Head Inn, Blackburn, 31.
Bull & Mouth Inn, London, 31.
Bullock Smithy, 48.
Buxton, Derbys., 31, 45, 46, 48.
Buxton Rd., Stockport, 85.

C

Calcutta, 35, 50, 75, 76, 91.
Caldbeck, Cumberland, 11.
Carlisle, 10, 13, 15, 30.
Carnforth Building & Gas Co., 73.
Carpenters' Hall, 63.
Charter, The, newspaper, 64.
Castle Hotel, Potteries, 31.
Castle & Falcon, Newark, 31.
Castle House, Hampton-on-Thames,
    89.

About the Author

Alan Richardson qualified as a veterinary surgeon in 1963 and pursued a career in veterinary research. He has also taken a serious interest in certain aspects of Roman archaeology and has published over 30 peer-reviewed papers on Roman roads, military camps, forts, surveys and field systems. In 1985 he was awarded the Reginald Taylor Prize by the British Archaeological Association for his work on the Roman penetration of East Cheshire.

Also from Humanities-Ebooks.co.uk

Stuart Andrews, *Methodism and Society*

Robert Johnson, *The British Empire: Pomp, Power and Postcolonialism*

Colin Nicholson, *Fivefathers: Interviews with late Twentieth-Century Scottish Poets*

Pamela Perkins, ed., *Francis Jeffrey's Highland and Continental Tours**

Keith Sagar, *D. H. Lawrence: Poet**

Irene Wiltshire, ed. *Letters of Mrs Gaskell's Daughters, 1856–1914**

* These titles are also available in print using links from
http://www.humanities-ebooks.co.uk